Gradus ad Parnassum

(Steps to perfection)

Know thyself; then thou shalt know the universe
and god

                    -      Pythagoras

The power of choice is responsibility

-Manly P. Hall

He that walks with a wise man shall be wise, but

a companion of fools shall be destroyed

-Proverbs 13:20

"We are living in the age of awakening. Be a

part of it.

Dare to think differently"

-P.R.C

Table of Contents

Part 3: Self Observation

1. Choices – Choosing Wisely and
   self-reflection

2. Words to embody and live by

   - Effort

   - Action

   - Will

   - Perseverance

   - Fortitude

   - Integrity

   - Love

3. Overcoming self-destructive
   Behaviors

4. Overcoming past failures and inner
   Conflicts

Part 4: Caveats

1. Mind states and feelings to avoid

- Laziness

- Envy

- Dishonesty

- Complacence

- Guilt

- Negative Thoughts

- Negative Feelings

2. Types of people to avoid

Part 5: Self-Modification

1. Re-inventing yourself

2. Overcoming fear of change

3. Being realistic

2) Social Responsibility

   (1) Our Responsibilities to the poor

   (2) Our Responsibilities to the sick

   (3) Our Responsibilities to the weak

   (4) Our Responsibilities to the old

   (5) Our Responsibilities to the young

   (6) Our Responsibilities to our society

3) Global responsibility

   (1) Our Responsibility to our

       immediate environment

   (2) Our Responsibility to our

       Global environment

Part 8: Epilogue

Heed these words, you who wish to probe the

depths of nature: If you do not find within

yourself that which you seek, neither will you

find it outside. If you ignore the wonders of

your own house, how do you expect to find

other wonders? In you is hidden the treasure of

treasures. Know Thyself and you will know the

Universe and the Gods

-    Delphic Oracle

<u>**Foreword**</u>

If you have opened this book with the expectation of reading another discourse on Pseudo psychology, then I regret to inform you that you have been mistaken. The instant text does not delve into new age thought but seeks to engage in another great science: The science of living through creative intent. Living with creative intent delves into the fine art of Creating your reality and doing so responsibly.

The fundamental premise espoused here is humanity possesses a great power of which lies the key to solving all problems of life. This power is the power of choice. Through the power you have in choosing from a multitude of options used to create your reality, you can consciously and intentionally manifest specific desires and experiences of your own choosing.

This eradicates chance, luck, coincidence, and fate. You will make life happen as you want it to. As an artist creates the pictures he desires through specific strokes of a brush on the easel, you will become the artist painting the picture of your life. It will be as you want it to be. All being done through specific choices intended to bring about a desired end.

The steps generated are based on basic forms of thought and behavior which aid you developing the ability to shape and form life as you choose. Most procedures are simple and basic but are necessary as our techno-industrial age has done away with the simple and basic in lieu of more complex forms of learning. This is sad as it is the mastery of the basics that provide the foundation for advancement along more complex lines of achievement.

If you have not taken the time to master the basics of living, then the more complex forms of life are experienced in an unprepared state. This increases the likelihood that many irreversible errors will occur, hindering your progress in life. Unfortunately, we all get one chance to get it right, so it would be in your best interest to prepare yourself as much as possible to get it right the first time.

Life does not come with instructions. Considering this truth, the Author will bring you back to the basics, giving you the opportunity to master them. You will then face life with the strength and confidence necessary to live successfully.

The concepts presented derive from studies of Sociology, Psychology, Philosophy, Biology, Hermetic Science, law, and empirical data obtained from observations of numerous social environments and the people who inhabit them in their natural state of function.

The teachings have come from applying the concepts set forth, and the experience of positive and successful results. Living with creative intent works. Your belief in this will not negate its verity. The laws of reality do not change simply because you do not believe in them. In any event the goal is not to harbor your beliefs or to proselytize in this philosophical and practical way to approach life, but to help you nurture and develop the belief in yourself as a powerful creative force in your life.

The author wishes to grant you the opportunity to generate and nurture the latent creative force within you by providing the tools which will allow you to use this gift given by the original source of all our creation.

This force bears within it the attributes of the principle source of creation. One attribute is the ability to create. The key to controlling and utilizing this power to create is choice. The choice made must be made with conscience awareness according to reality.

The caveats involved are that you bear the sole responsibility of the consequences of your choices, and its created effects. If you are strong enough, confident enough, and wise enough to

attempt to wield this power in your life in a
positive and responsible way, then turn the page
and learn of the art and wisdom of living with
Creative intent. This will take you to the ultimate
pinnacle of true living and success, if you so
choose…

INTRODUCTION

I.	What is Creative Intent?

Creative Intent is a guide that teaches you to take full responsibility for your life. The results lead to an increase in control over what events you want to manifest in your life. You will have power to manifest what you want to occur or experience in life.

The text begins with a five-part guide geared towards engaging in subjective self-analysis, and introspection. The first five-parts are intended to bring about specific modifications in thought and behavior. The aim is to change lifelong habits that govern your behavior. Once the subjective habitual thought patterns are changed, then the objective behavior will change. This will lead to a change in effects and circumstances in your life. What changes are experienced depend on what you have changed about yourself.

The self-analysis is also designed to raise your consciousness. An increase in consciousness allows you to act in harmony with truth and reality by making choices consistent to what really is, and not what is perceived to be. Our perceptions are sometimes skewed by our personal beliefs and bias. This leads to faulty decision making. The truth is what you experience in life is based upon the choices you make. Unfortunately, it is also true that it is the result of the choices others make as well.

Your character is made up of those experiences and the effects thereof on your psycho-emotional make-up. You are what you experience. It would be in your best interest to control what you experience, your perception of that experience, and be aware of the choice made that brought it about.

Once you comprehend this concept, you will know that you are wholly responsible for what, who, where, how, and why you are. With careful observation, you can and will see you are responsible for your life through the choices made.

The first five parts of the program are Awareness, Activity, Self-Observation, Caveats, and Self-Modification. Part six consist of a practical approach to applying the content learned in the first five parts. Part seven emphasizes three different forms of responsibility that must be known for you to get a grasp on how important your role and behavior is in the grander scheme of life.

All that you do influences all that exist. Everything is connected in this universe. Your actions are akin to throwing a pebble in a pond. It creates a ripple effect that travels on until it is stopped by another force. Part 8 contains a personal message of inspiration from the author to you with the hope of encouraging you to become stronger, wiser, and heart-centered.

The main objective of this book is to help the reader comprehend the importance of taking full responsibility of the choices made; once this is done you will be able to create the best quality of life for yourself. The quality of life you create comes from the understanding that if you must bear the burden of your choices, then you will exercise more caution in the decision-making process.

You will therefore make better choices to increase the positive effects and reduce the negative. Anyone who wants to improve themselves can. The first step in doing so is to choose to do so knowing the responsibility of such is yours and yours alone.

II.   Who is it for?

Everyone is not ready to accept the responsibility for creating their life. So, who is it for? Let us start with the understanding that there are two types of people in the world: People of action and everyone else. This book is for people of action. It is for those who are willing to be brutally honest with them-selves. It is for people who are willing to face and acknowledge long held misbeliefs about who they are. It is for those who are willing to rid themselves of the automatic defense mechanisms that arise in the face of unpleasant truths. It is for those who want to cease being in denial, repressing, transferring emotions and thoughts, regressing to childlike states and being dishonest to avoid facing up to a difficult situation or truth in their life.

Developing the ability to accurately assess and confront issues one has avoided is an essential element in this process. You have to address the causes in life. This ability rids the barriers that have prohibited you from adequately resolving those issues and eliminating their negative effects on your life.   Once life's issues are confronted and resolved in an honest way, the barrier they posed towards progress is removed.

Living with creative intent is for those who are willing to accept the truth that life is a continuous learning lesson, where class is conducted everywhere, and the education taught is in real time. You learn, apply, and experience simultaneously. You learn through experience, assimilate the meaning of each experience, and then conduct yourself accordingly. This is the basis of true wisdom.

Living with creative intent is for those who understand that success or failure in life is a matter of choice. If you are unable to learn from your experiences, then you will fail to move beyond the point of which you've learned from your last experience.

The direct consequence of this is that specific occurrences will continually arise in your life until you adequately address them. You must discover the cause, address it, and learn from it. This act thereby eliminates the recurring event from your life. You will then move forward from it or with it in a positive manner.

If you don't, the event will always pop-up at an inopportune time, essentially holding you a slave to it, and keeping you stuck in that point of your life.

Taking responsibility for your choices and the effects of them is necessary for the program to have its full effect. Living with creative intent is not for the dishonest, mediocre, and weak-willed person. It is not for those who believe all should come easy and have no desire to strive for a better life.

It is not for the person who believes all should come easily. If you do not or are not willing to comply with the strict mandates of the program, you will not receive the full benefit of it. Living with creative intent modifies thought patterns, behavior, and replaces self-destructive and less beneficial behaviors with more productive modes of thought and behavior.

It acts as a form of self-cognitive behavioral therapy. Your actions are addressed by addressing your thoughts. The mind is like a computer. For you to get the most from it, you must put the best into it. It is then your mind will produce better solutions to life's problems.

This will bring about better responses to each of life's dilemmas as they arise. Only the strong, willing, and mature adults' who are ready to face life as it is, and not through a comfortable perception, will achieve success and great results from the program. All else who fall short of this mandate will fail.

III.   The goal of living with creative intent

The goal of living With Creative Intent is to help you develop the strength of character necessary to face life's occurrences effectively. This generation is disconnected from the natural law principle of cause and effect. This principle states for every choice and action made or inaction taken; there occurs a logical series of events that bring about an opposite and equal reaction. The series of reactions correspond to the original cause.

It is not possible for you to free yourself from the responsibility of experiencing the effects of the causes you have put in motion. Religious and scientific literatures have supported this fact. The concept of "as ye sow, so shall ye reap" of the Christian Bible had explained this fact.

Sir Isaac Newton, when studying the laws of nature realized this truth and revealed its operation in the statement that for every action there is an equal and opposite reaction.

A person can do nothing in life that would free them from the responsibility they must take for the effects of their actions. Man's law of limited liability and attempts at avoidance are a sham in the face of this fact. One cannot avoid, run from, or buy their way out of having to accept responsibility for the causes they have put in motion.

If you have done wrong doing right will not relinquish the effects of the wrong you have done. Doing right will only bring about a response that may mitigate the effects of the wrong but will never absolve them altogether.

However drastic this seems you need not worry if the causes you put in motion are aligned with the desired outcome. The knowledge of this truth will help lead you to true success and prosperity in life. Whatever desires are in your mind and heart can be made manifest in your life by setting into motion causes that correspond with the affects you desire in your life. Your fate is truly within your hands, or better said within your choices.

Your life is shaped by the choices you make. The choices must be made consciously with awareness of the specific effect that will be brought about. On the other hand, your life is also affected by the choices of others. Not only do you have to be careful about your own choices, but also careful of the choices made by others.

This way you don't suffer the ill consequences of someone else's bad choices. This will be studied later. The overall consequence of the practice is that you will increase power over your life, and everything that happens in it. If this concept were known, accepted, understood, and lived by the human species not only could everyone change their own lives for the better, but will also change the quality of life on the planet as well.

The effect would be a higher quality of life for all people. The state of our planet's health would improve as well. The focus is to increase the quality of your life by improving the self through a process of character development that starts

from the inside.

The choices you make will be made in conscious

awareness of what you want to happen. This is

what living with creative intent is.

PART 1

AWARENESS

What is necessary to change a person is to change his awareness of himself.

\- Abraham Maslow

1. Being honest

This above all: to thine own self be true, and it must follow, as the night the day, thou canst not then be false to any man.

-William Shakespeare

There is always the question of whether honesty is the best policy when dealing with another person. Hurting another's feelings or causing trouble are factors that exist in this debate. However, when dealing with your-self, honesty must be the only policy no matter what the truth may be.

It is a natural defense mechanism to deny, distort, or alter unpleasant truths to avoid the thoughts and feelings that are provoked by them. Evolution has allowed humans this fail-safe mechanism of denial to help us cope with circumstances that cause psychological disturbances. Nature has endowed us with cognitive dissonance.

When a person is faced with a reality they cannot cope with, or conflicts with strongly held beliefs of self or others, then a lie is useful in alleviating the mental and emotional tension created from those unpleasant truths. Self-deceit is a useful tool when dealing with reality becomes too difficult.

It is not easy to be completely honest with your-self. This is even truer when it concerns being honest in the face of undesirable character traits, situations, and the poor effects of bad choices. The truth is seen only in the way narcotic and alcoholic anonymous groups begin their workshops for new members.

Each new member must stand in front of the group and admit that they have a problem and identify themselves with the problem. You must stand up and admit to yourself the truth about yourself no matter what that truth may be and identify with that.

Being brutally honest is the first step in creating your life. It is the most important step to take. You will never be able to improve yourself, bad traits, or the circumstances in your life unless you can be brutally honest with yourself about who you are.

Take a moment and think of your life and yourself. Are you living life the way you want? Are you who you think you are? Are your friends who you think they are? If what you believe yourself to be and what you believe your life to be is inconsistent with what it truly is, then you must ask yourself why it is that way.

Ask yourself this question and be honest about it. Once you have completed an accurate description of yourself, reflect on your past. Do not reflect on the past to ruminate upon it. Reflect on it in an introspective manner analyzing all events and circumstance you have experienced. Again, this must be done in truth and honesty.

Remember the choices you have made. Remember how you treated yourself and thought about yourself. Remember how you have treated others and thought about others. Look at how you dealt with situations and see if it was with a cool head or cold heart. Remember the environments you were in and the people you were around. Think of how all this influenced you.

When you analyze your past, it is meant in every sense of the word. Dissect your life into bits and pieces.

Follow a linear and logical order from your earliest remembered experiences up until the most present. The purpose of this is to bring to your awareness the reality of your life, and how you got there. This reality will be based upon the series of events that occurred from the past to the present.

You will also find patterns in this series of events. You will discover patterns of behavior that you repeatedly engage in. It doesn't matter where you are or how old you are. These patterns of behavior are a part of you and define who you are. They also define the life you live and what you experience. These patterns are your character traits. What you will discover is the choices you have made are based upon the character traits you have developed over a course of time by repeatedly responding to situations in the same manner you always have.

Your character traits have led you into a pattern of behavior that has either proven to be beneficial or detrimental depending on the type of decisions that have been made over a period. Your traits have led you into a pattern of decision making that automatically recur whenever similar situations arise at different points in your life. This is what must be changed.

Decisions made must not be made impulsively or unconsciously, but with conscious intent. Impulsive decision making reduces the availability of positive options in life and increases the likelihood of a bad choice being made that may have a resonating effect well into your future. This could be very difficult to remove or remedy.

Upon close examination, you will see patterns of choices that led to good in your life, and patterns of choices that led to bad. You will also see patterns in the type of personal and social relationships you consistently engage in that will reflect the type of people and social situations you find yourself in. From your intimate relationships, your friends, the type of work you do, and associates you have around you will discover a similarity between them all despite the difference in time and place.

You will find yourself in similar environments time and again, and in similar situations over a period though the faces and places may be different. These patterns of behavior, environmental circumstances, and associations are constantly created and recreated through your thoughts, decisions, and personal characteristics that draw you to these circumstances and realities.

Think of the choices you made in life that led you to situations that were favorable and beneficial. Continue to make those decisions and similar ones. Think of the choices that led you to unfavorable circumstances. Stop making those choices. It's that simple. It just requires a modicum of awareness of your-self and behaviors as well as the requisite will to make changes in your decision making.

The purpose of self-analysis and introspective awareness is to help you comprehend why you are at where you're at and how you got there. This knowledge is the first key to self-empowerment. Now you know why your life is the way it is. You know it is not the result of bad luck or circumstances beyond your control.

It is not chance or fate that led you to your present circumstances, but upon things you had some if not all control over. You are where you are at because it is you who put yourself there. The sum of your life is the direct result of the choices you have made. This is an incredible truth as it gives you the definite power to guide and control your fate from here on. You now know you are master and commander of your fate.

The power that steers the path of your life lies within your choices. You can make your life what you want it to be. It all starts this moment. It begins right now with the choices you make. You must be conscious of this fact and not believe or have faith that it is true. You must know it is true. Most importantly of all you must be honest with your-self every step of the way.

2.   Accepting Responsibility

*The real freedom of any individual can always
be measured by the amount of responsibility
which he must assume for his own welfare and
security.*

-Robert Welch

By this time, you should be aware of what
stage of life you are at, and how you have gotten
there. The next step is to accept responsibility for
it all. It seems like a heavy burden, doesn't it? It
is because it is. The weight of this responsibility
is necessary to temper the character getting it
ready for the processes you must engage in from
this point on. Just imagine you had to admit to all
your faults, mistakes, bad acts, and irresponsible
behavior each time it occurred; and had to accept
immediate and complete responsibility for the
consequences of each act.

If your life could be read like an open book you would be very careful of the content you placed within that book, wouldn't you. You would be conscious of how you spoke, ate, and acted towards your-self and others, and how you allowed others to treat you. All would see you in rare and real form during each of these moments; Passing judgment each step of the way. It would immediately be decided whether you were right or wrong and what consequence should be meted out.

The response would be instant. You would, under these circumstances, weigh your decisions more carefully for fear of doing something that would show you in an unfavorable light, or bring about unfavorable circumstances. Who would, in this scenario, want to be viewed as a bad or irresponsible person? It's fair to say that no one would.

It is a natural human impulse to focus on the good of one-self and look for the best qualities while hiding less favorable ones. If you knew you would have to admit to and accept responsibility for the bad, suffer direct and immediate consequences derived therefrom, then you would be much more cautious, wise, and thoughtful in your decision making. You would use the foresight and patience necessary to make better decisions.

This is the purpose of having to accept full responsibility for your choices and consequences. It acts as a deterrent to making rash, hasty, and bad decisions that could harm you and others. If everyone in this world knew they are completely responsible for the choices they make and the consequences therefrom, then a lot of things would be done differently.

Most people would cease to engage in indiscriminate decision-making without regard to the effects. There is no doubt you would be more careful as well. This type of scenario turns everyday life into a challenge where the wrong choice could be fatal. This is good. By default, you will be careful about the things you choose to do. This will change the course of events in your life.

Positive experiences will occur because you made better decisions. Better choices lead to better outcomes. Be smart. Choose wisely. Things will get better. Be foolish, and it is guaranteed things will get worse. No matter the situation, you are responsible for it. This is the message. This concept is not governed by the laws of man, but upon the natural law of Cause and effect. This law ensures every action receives its equal re-action.

This ensures universal harmonic equilibrium is maintained allowing for the continued existence of all within its creation. You could compare it to universal homeostasis. Balance must be kept. We are bound by this law whether we know it or not, and whether we like it or not. You will suffer the consequences of your actions. It cannot be avoided. No matter the situation, you are responsible for it.

4) Knowing what you want

"The first step in getting what you want, is knowing what you want"

- Arthur D. Hlavaty

A greater knowledge of self, coupled with the power of conscious intent, reason, and truth, has prepared you to take the next step. This is the phase of conscious direction. This phase is guided by your innermost desires and wants from life. At this stage, you will discover what you really want from life or who you want to be in that life. Your desires, needs, and wants will guide your choices from here on. So, the first and essential question you must ask before beginning this part of the process is: What do you want?

Most people are asked this in youth with questions such as what you want to be when you grow up, and who do you want to be when you grow up and we answer these questions with the quintessential children's answers like "I want to be a fireman, or a policeman". I think as we all get older we forget this enthusiastic zeal felt during youth at the possibility of becoming someone, or something that is part of the greater scheme of life unknown at youth.

With age comes the impact of reality that collides against the aspirations and dreams of our youth. It sometimes damages these dreams and allows for a silent acceptance of fate against the weight of our hearts desire. So, the young and jubilant child that wants the best of the world slowly resigns him, or her-self to becoming another cog in the wheel of the machine that governs our lives and existence. We forget what we want in life in exchange for a means of sustenance that merely helps us get by.

This is the greatest mistake you could make. You must never forget what you want in life, nor must you accept your current circumstances as set in stone. You can become more and obtain more in life. Life is the equivalent of abundance. Look at nature who gives so freely and abundantly of her-self.

We, as organic and conscious manifestations of nature, bear within us this ability to create, to do so in abundance, and receive like kind in return. Knowing what you want in life is the first step in instituting this power to create. Knowing what you want will define the choices you make, and the choices you make will define what you create.

The pilot flies the plane; the Captain steers the ship; the executive closes the deal; and the athlete wins the race. These are examples of those who knew what they wanted to accomplish and did it. They made the choices necessary to achieve it. It is time to ask yourself the question you may not have asked your-self since childhood. What do you want to be? Who do you want to be? Where do you want to be? Who are you? How can you get there? What do you need to do to prepare?

These questions and many more are essential to this part of the process. If you have never given thought to any of this, or have not done so in a while, then now is the time to do so. If possible, take a moment to do so right now. This moment, and every moment from here on end completely depend upon this.

Your future depends on this. Remember, your future is the sum of the choices made in the present. Those choices should and must be geared toward helping to bring about the desired end. It's like playing chess, but in real life. In the game of chess, you must think of every step you make, and do so at least three steps ahead of your opponent to ensure that your desire (to capture the king) is fulfilled.

Your opponent in this game is life itself. You must think of all your moves at least three to five steps in advance, ensuring each step moves you further without suffering setbacks. The king in this game is your goal. You know where you are at. You know how you got there. Now you must take the time to figure out where you want to go from here. Have a clear vision.

Imagine it first. Using your imagination is an integral part of the process. How can you ever picture yourself doing or being something when you have never pictured your-self doing or being it? Ideas are the bedrock of planning and organizing your life. All ideas first develop in your imagination. Imagination is the key in helping envision the process with the desired end.

You can see and experience everything you want before it all occurs. Without a clear vision and certainty of what you want in life, you will be like a leaf in the wind on a late and windy fall day. You will be blown to wherever the wind takes you. You will be a pawn to nature. Subject to her every whim. This is not what you want. You want complete control over your life.

Now mind you it is impossible to control every aspect of your life as it is intertwined with the lives of billions of other people who have their own interest in mind, and who will use you to further those interests. However, you do want the most control over your-self and your circumstances. Having control gives you great power over the will of others seeking to advance their interest and gives you the strength necessary to withstand external forces that will use you.

Knowing what you want is akin to being behind the rudder steering your-self down the path you want to go. Thus, you will naturally develop more power over manifesting the exact circumstances you want to experience in your life. This eliminates chance, luck, and fate from your life.

Fortune favors the bold, and opportunity opens its doors for those who knock knowing what they want and aren't afraid to go get it. Be the one who knocks on the door of opportunity, breaking it down if necessary to pave the way to your success. Take the steps necessary to achieve your goals. Know what you want and go get it. Start now. It all starts with the thought of what you want, envisioning your-self doing it, and going out there and making it happen. Choose your success. You and only you alone are responsible for making it happen.

5) Pragmatism

"Pragmatism is good prevention for problems"

-Amit Kalantri

Knowing what you want and making the choice to pursue that goal are two great qualities to develop. However, you must also take into consideration other factors when conducting this exercise. The primary factor you must deal with is reality. You must be realistic when deciding what you want.

This means you must decide to do something that can reasonably be accomplished. For example, if you do not have a voice that can produce harmonic notes, then it would not be wise to try and become a vocal singer (at least not for public display).

However, if your desire is to truly make great music, then you may be able to write music, play music, or even try some software that could help. The point is you must know fully well your capabilities, strengths and weaknesses. There are ways to live your dreams. To begin with, you must understand all the elements involved in the process including yourself and your abilities.

Then you must make a choice consistent with the data derived from this analysis. There is something for everyone. Take a moment and look to find your own niche in the crooks of the world. The following are a short, and certainly not limitedly defined, set of steps to consider and follow when engaging in this process. You can always make your own determinations and decisions when developing a method that helps in the creative process.

Everyone has their own method of doing things. Whether another agrees or disagrees with it doesn't matter. If it works for you, doesn't hurt anyone else, and produces the results you are looking for then by all means do what works. First you must look at your health. Are you capable, physically, of carrying out the task you sought for your-self?

Second, how is your mental health? I am not talking about whether you have a psychological deficiency (If you do it should be considered), but whether your mind is clear enough now to focus on the task you set out for your-self. If your mind is full of thoughts of ill things from the past or personal problems that draw your attention away from what you should be focused on, then it is recommended you sort out all personal issues that may muddle your mind.

Your mind must be free of all negative content. Otherwise the imaginative and rational processes needed to map out your life's plan will be hindered. It's like when your phone or Desktop has too much information, and not enough memory to store or manage all the data, the computers start to run slow. Programs stall, and even shut down not allowing you to continue with the task you had to do. The same thing happens when you have too much stuff on your mind. It slows down.

Third, get to know your-self. Are you industrious, Creative, Dependable? Or, are you lazy, un-imaginative, and un-reliable? Make a list of your weaknesses, strengths, and habits. Include any other aspect of your-self that others may reveal to you that either helps or hurts. Both are equally valuable in discovering who you are.

The choice should align with your strengths, with weaknesses kept in mind. Always be realistic. Do not try to do something you are not strong enough to complete. If your weaknesses become too much, then you must engage in a process of strengthening your weaknesses. If you are still unable to, find something else you can do.

Fourth, you must determine what you are willing to do. Know what you are willing to sacrifice, learn, pay for, and even struggle for. Nothing in life is free. Everything has its price. The greater the thing desired, the higher the price.

The price isn't always a financial one. Sometimes it requires an extraordinary amount of effort and will to obtain. Sometimes it requires a personal sacrifice, and sometimes it is about money.

The age-old aphorism "it takes money to make money" is just as true now as it was in the past. At this point you should know who you are, what you want to do, what you're willing to do, and what you can do. Half the task is done. A pragmatic approach is the most realistic approach in getting your desires to match your abilities.

Part 2

Action

Ex Nihilo Nihil Fit

(From nothing, nothing is produced)

I.   Goal Setting

*"If you want to live a happy life, tie it to a goal,
not
to people or things."*

– Albert Einstein

It is good to know what you want, but this means nothing if you take no action to get it. The most crucial part of the entire process of taking control of your life is taking the action necessary to make it come about. Action is the activity that is critical to obtaining success.

Plan all you want, take no action upon that plan and nothing will come of it. Faith without works is dead. You must make happen what you have planned for your-self. The first step to help make this happen is to set goals. What you want is your goal.

The next step is to find out how to achieve that goal. Then you must plan the steps necessary to bring about the completion of that goal. Goals are your best friends. In all reality, they have been the best friends to all those who have succeeded in life. All those who win have had a goal set toward winning. All winners have goals.

Racers have the finish line. Football players have the touchdown. Pilots have their destination. College students have the degree. In all successes, there is a goal involved. There is always something to aspire to. What also comes along with all of this is a defining moment that places value on the progress made and marks the level of achievement obtained.

A person who treads through life without goals will be like a basketball player who has no rim on the court. He would be running up and

down the court with no aim or end in sight, and

no advancement in any way. They are not even

in the game. Setting up a game plan is the next

step.

II.   Planning

"By failing to prepare, you are preparing to fail."

— Benjamin Franklin

Having a plan is the beginning of the process of achieving your goal. Look at sports such as basketball and football. The overall goal is to gain more points than the other team before the time runs out in the game. The team with the most points wins.

On the sideline's coaches can be seen with clipboards containing papers that outline how their team will get the most points, and what plays are most effective in doing so. These planned strategies are the key in advancing toward the desired end, and that end is to win.

These plays are called the game-plan. This is what you need for your life. You need a game plan. Whatever your desires, they can be obtained through the use and execution of a carefully constructed game plan. It is a systematic process based on what's necessary to achieve the goal. This process must be based upon the exact knowledge necessary to obtain and achieve your goal.

First decide what you want. Then investigate and do research to learn how to obtain it. Third, take the information you have gathered and organize it into a logical, linear, and step-by-step process geared towards achieving your goal. Finally, follow the format you laid out until you have completed it. This is a game plan. Plan thoroughly, obtain as much information as you can, and stick to the plan.

Do not deviate unless it is necessary to adjust. There will be times when you might have to modify the plan just a little to compensate for unknown variables that may interfere. Do not give up. Do not lose your nerve halfway through. If it gets difficult, keep going. Nothing in life worth having is ever easy to obtain. Do not get discouraged at difficulty. It is supposed to be like that. That is why it is a process.

III.   Taking action

-Roger Babson

Setting a goal and developing a plan to obtain that goal is not enough. The next step in the process, and most crucial, is to act upon that intent. Physical action is necessary in the process of achievement. You cannot wish your dreams into existence despite what any self-help book or guru seminar speaker may say to you. It just won't happen. You can attract to you that of which you desire by continuously paying mind to it, but you still must engage in some sort of physical action to help it manifest in your life.

You can plan and wish all you want. However, if you do not act with what is necessary to make that plan come to life, then it will not happen. Your goal will be nothing but a fantasy, and your dreams but castles in the air. For your reality to become what you want it to be, you must make it that way. You do so by actively engaging in the process that is necessary to bring that about. Life is not passive. It is active. Activity is what allows life to occur.

Activity is the masculine creative aspect of life of which you possess. It does not matter whether you're a man or woman. Both possess the active ability to create. Action is the essence of life. It is movement. It is the combination of two or more factors to help produce a new outcome. One creates nothing. Acting with conscious intent to bring about a specific outcome is what you need to do here.

Once you act to create your life the chances of whatever you're working on coming to fruition are increased exponentially. One thing you must remember from here on end is that this process will produce many different things that may hinder your progress. For every action, there is an equal and opposite reaction to counterbalance the act made. It is just the universes way of keeping balance with itself.

This is called resistance. This may seem like a bad thing. It's not. Resistance in life can be your best friend or greatest enemy depending on how you approach it. To the weightlifter resistance is a great friend for it is the tincture that produces the mix to stronger muscles. Resistance in this context is what are commonly known as obstacles.

IV.   Overcoming Obstacles

"Obstacles do not block the path, they are the path"

-Author unknown

Obstacles always arise and interfere with your progress. The nature of an obstacle is to challenge the progress made in some way. Otherwise it would not be an obstacle. Do not become upset, discouraged, or frustrated when you come across these. Obstacles are a necessary and unavoidable part of the process.

It is recommended you do not develop negative feelings or thoughts regarding the obstacles you encounter in life. Instead, embrace the process and obstacles that come along as an indication you are on the right path, and as an opportunity to detect any flaws inherent in your plan.

It is good to detect flaws in your plan before you get too far into it. The failure to do so may lead to a point where it will be too late to address. Obstacles are an indicator something is wrong. It's like getting a headache or not feeling well. These are ways your body will tell you something is not functioning right. An obstacle says, "Check out what is going on right now because you may be on the verge of making an error, and I am thwarting your efforts as a result".

Obstacles allow you to make the necessary adjustments at an early stage of the process to ensure the best results are reached. Obstacles ensure you remain on the path toward great results. You will not achieve your goal without overcoming obstacles. When you do, any obstacle encountered is turned into a stepping stone that brings you closer to your goal.

The concept is akin to the age-adage that when life throws lemons at you, you make lemon-aid. Take a moment to think of the runner in the hurdled race. The runners race down the track at top speed. At some point in the race they encounter several hurdles in their path. What do they do? Do they slow down and stop? Do they cry and say they can't go on with these obstacles in their way?

None of the above; upon seeing the hurdles in their way they speed up, gain momentum, and at just the right moment thrust themselves over the hurdle. They do this repeatedly until they have passed all of them and continue to finish the race.

They never stop. They never falter. They never waiver for one instant; they keep going despite the obstacles in their way.

This is the mindset you must have in life. Every path taken will have its obstacles. See them for what they are, know why they are present, and determine how you can best overcome them; after that continue your journey. By the time you have reached the end of it all, not only will you have succeeded, but you will also be all the stronger because of what you have gone through to get there.

You will be all the wiser because of all you had to learn, and go through, to get to where you're at. You will have become a better and stronger person because of all the adversity and struggle you had to go through for you to get to where you want to be. Obstacles are a good thing if you know how to address them. But you must address them.

If you ignore the obstacles, or warning signs something is wrong, then you will most likely suffer a major setback at a time where you most cannot afford it. All issues must be addressed. Nothing just goes away on its own. Face the obstacles in your life and then move on to your desired end.

<u>Part 3</u>

<u>Self-Observation</u>

"The unexamined life

Is not worth living"

-Socrates

1. Choices

"We are our choices"

— Jean-Paul Sartre

The importance of the choices you make in your life has been addressed in the first part of the program. It is addressed again because of how important, and crucial it is to your overall ability to creating your life. It is imperative you comprehend with complete understanding the trajectory of events, and experiences in your life are directly correlated to the choices you make. It is even connected to the choices you don't make. Each choice made is another rail in the track guiding your life. Each choice adds to the direction you are going. This is true no matter how big or small the choice may be.

Be aware of the choices you make. No matter how you try to avoid it the full weight of responsibility for the choice made rest upon you. It is best to use reason rather than emotion when you make your choice. A reasonable mind is always best suited to make an accurate assessment of the scenario. It is also suited to determine the best course of action to take in response.

Reasonable minds make reasonable choices. Choices made under the throws of an emotional fit oft times turn out to be detrimental. Cooler heads do prevail. Young children act under emotion because their reasoning faculties have yet to develop. You are not a young child. You are an adult. As such you are held responsible for your actions. Children lack the ability to discern right from wrong and don't think through the consequence of their actions.

Adults, on the other hand can discern right from wrong. You must use this power to make the best choice for you, and always take into consideration how the choice will affect you, others, and your environment. Discussions about this portion of living with creative intent will be discussed later. The next chapter will review certain characteristics that are necessary for your advancement. There are certain character traits you must develop in order to live with creative intent. In slang, it is called stepping your game up.

6) Words to Embody and live by

1. Effort

2. Action

3. Will

4. Perseverance

5. Fortitude

6. Integrity

7. Love

If you are wondering why it is so important to comprehend and embody the essence of these words the reason is this: any action or choice made in accordance with the spirit and meaning of these words increases the likelihood of the successful achievement of your endeavors, and ability to manifest your desires in life.

All actions are of a positive nature when made in this light. These concepts are simple. Yet the most profound truths and powerful forces in life are found in the simpler aspects of it all. Take in mind the vast source of all our technological achievements operates upon a binary code system consisting of only two numbers.

Despite the simplicity of their meaning, it appears to be difficult for many to practice these concepts in their everyday affairs. Understand that easy does not do it. Difficult is only difficult because you have yet to master the thing that is presently difficult. Once you master a difficult thing it becomes easy. Let's closely look at these words so that you may begin to see the importance of them in your life.

1. Effort:

> "Exertion, endeavor; also: a product of effort. Active or applied force."

The first part of this definition emphasizes a concept known as exertion. Exertion as a requisite part of effort is very important. Exertion is a verb that means to put into action. As you can see effort begins with action. The effort to obtain something that is desired, whatever it may be, begins with taking some form of action. For example: I am putting the effort into writing this book by actively writing the words down and continuing to do so until the text is finished with the desire to produce a book that will be read by you. I am making this effort with the hope it will have a positive impact upon your life.

I have heard so many stories from people who say they do not get what they want out of life. However, after paying close attention to what is said, and comparing it to what steps the person has taken to get the thing desired, it has been realized the individual has not made the requisite effort to reach their goal.   This is the cause to why they never get what they want. They don't work for it.

Things cannot be wished into existence. A desire in and of itself is insufficient without action and effort behind it. Think of a person who wants to shed some unwanted weight. The desire is present. However, if that person makes no changes in the diet, nor begins an exercise regimen that is geared toward reducing the fat in the body, that individual will never lose the weight.

This person does want to lose weight but makes no effort to do so. What do you think is going to happen? Nothing will happen. No weight will be lost, and that person will continue to be in a state of unfulfilled desire. It must be known that unfulfilled desires are the basis of many neurotic disorders. To avoid hurting yourself mentally you must do what you say you will do.

Effort must be made and can only be made by the individual. That means you are the only one who can and is supposed to do what you want to have done in your life. No one else can make the effort for you. And if you think you can get others to do the work for you without putting in effort, just understand that the mere act of getting others to do work for you is an effort all on its own.

In life you must make the necessary effort to bring about and manifest your hearts desires. No one is going to do for you what you need to do for your-self. Moreover, no one will do it like you would. I believe you may have heard the age-adage "If you want something done right, you have to do it your-self". This maxim is pregnant with philosophical truths that have withstood the test of time.

You are responsible for you. You are responsible for your own well-being, and as such must actively engage in a constant process of effort to ensure you experience that well-being no matter the form it takes. You are the active force that makes it all happen, and you will receive the best results from all your effort by putting in 100%. It may seem like 100% is un-attainable, but anything less is un-acceptable.

Halfhearted attempts are futile. You're building the house of your life. How sturdy, comfortable, and long-lasting it will be, depends on the amount of effort you put into it. Always keep this in mind. Constant effort does not necessarily entail you work harder. You can work smarter. You will receive results just as good if not better. Always keep in mind the following: You will get out of your endeavors the same in amount and quality as you put in.

2. Action:

"The accomplishment of a thing usually over a period of time, in stages, or with the possibility of repetition."

Effort and action are relatively synonymous due to the fact they both entail structured activity with the aim of bringing about a specific end. However, the line that marks the difference between the two is the lasting process that takes place over a period. The main purpose of effort is to generate the energy necessary to fuel your actions over a span of time. Once the effort is made to act, alongside a structured and well-planned course of activity, the goals set will manifest in due time.

You will eventually reap the benefits of all your actions. Remember the following: "For every action there is an equal and opposite reaction", and "As ye' sow, so shall ye' reap". The second component of action is stages and repetition of action. This means that all actions are taken in a step-by-step process. This step-by-step process is followed by the repetition of the action that best suits the end desired.

For example, the light bulb in your lamp went out and you want to replace it. The first step would be to un-screw the old light bulb that does not work. The second step would be to get a new light bulb. The third step would be to screw in the new light bulb. The final step would be to turn the light on to see if the process was successful. If not, you would have to repeat the process.

This is a small example of the type of actions to be taken in your life. Everything must be taken

one step at a time. If the step you are taking put's
you back, then you are doing something wrong.
You should then re-evaluate your game-plan. All
actions must advance you to the next step. It
cannot be otherwise for otherwise equal's failure,
and failure is not an option. Taking action must
be a part of your character. Action means forward
movement towards your end. You must stay
active and continually use your efforts to do so.

3. Will:

"The mental powers manifesting as wishing,
choosing, desiring, or intending; A disposition
to act according to principles or ends; Power of
controlling one's own action's or emotion's; To
determine by an act of choice; decree, ordain,
intend, purpose; Also: choice."

As can be gleaned from the definition of the word will, its very nature encompasses all that has been taught thus far. What is being developed in character through this program is the strengthening and proper development of the will. You are as strong as your will and all that you create will be as strong as the will expended during its creation. Will is a powerful word.

It is a mental force possessed by all human beings. It is used often and described by many. Unfortunately, not enough of the human population exerts enough will into their projects and endeavors.

It is recommended this natural faculty be developed and strengthened. You have been taught you have free will. But have you been taught how to use this will, or even what this will is?

This is one of the sources of ills on this planet: The ignorance of the nature of our will, and how to properly use the will in a responsible pro-creative manner. A conscious intelligent use of this will is an absolute requisite to your success. For you to succeed in life, you must have a strong will. Your will must be strong enough to control your thoughts, feelings and actions.

This is necessary to free your-self from the useless clutter of information that consumes your mind day in and day out. Your mind needs to be free as it is the controller of the will. Only thoughts geared toward your positive and adequate development should be allowed. Your speech, gait, conduct, breath, posture, and emotions must be controlled using your will.

Your will is developed through the conscious control over your acts. For example, if you have a bad habit of swearing, then you would have to use will power to catch your-self every-time you curse or are about to curse in order that you may prevent your-self from doing it. You can develop your will by learning new things and taking on tasks that seem difficult but can be done by you.

All acts that require strength of mind are essentially acts that build the will. This is what is meant by going the extra mile. If you were exercising for 45 minutes daily, then beginning an exercise regime that is 1 hour long would be an act of will.

This is because it challenges you to break free from a level of comfort to do something more. Continued acts of this nature will gradually render what was difficult to something of ease.

The reason for this is the will was strengthened to the point which made what was difficult, easy. Another act of building will power is getting in the habit of doing all you say you will do. You must likewise not do anything you say you wouldn't do. This will strengthen your word making it possible to create all you say you will do simply because you said you would.

The mind responds immediately as if it were a command, making the body do what was said.

Remember that there is a psycho-biological connection. The mind and body are one. Each one influences the other. Whatever the mind is focused on the body reacts to. Whatever the body feels the mind reacts to. Will power must be exercised like a muscle. After the eventual strengthening of this part of your character, you will notice that all you will to manifest will manifest.

4. Perseverance:

"To persist in an undertaking in spite of
difficulties."

The topic of obstacles was mentioned earlier,
as well as the importance of overcoming them
until the end. This is perseverance. It is during
times when the goals you have set yourself seem
un-obtainable, and life throws curveballs at you
that you must engage in the profound act of
persevering.

Perseverance means you keep on going.
Every human being who has walked this planet
has encountered some difficulty. Obstacles,
setbacks, and losses are a part of life. However,
their presence must not be viewed negatively.

These barriers do not exist to simply frustrate,
delay, hurt, or sabotage you, but also inform you

of points you may be overlooking. This was discussed earlier. They can educate you and strengthen you. They educate you as to what you are doing wrong and strengthen you with each experience you overcome. In the face of these realities you must continue until the end even if the present seems as if it's nowhere near that end.

Continue to persevere. Make the changes necessary to get you to the next step. Keep moving no matter the level of resistance. Complete the task no matter how hard. Know that if you persevere through it all, the day will come when you look up and your goal will be a reality.

5. Fortitude:

"Strength of mind that enables one to meet
danger or bear pain or adversity with courage."

Fortitude by its very nature entails strength
and power of the mind. This power of mind
allows you to overcome the psychological and
emotional pressures that rise during this journey.
Anguish,   heartbreak,   discouragement,
depression, and many other negative feelings
may be felt due to the difficulty of the process.
Life is not easy. We all need some way to cope
with and deal with the difficulty of living. We
also need a source of energy that could be used
to help move us through it. Fortitude is the energy
you need to succeed.

The road to riches and success is paved with danger. If it were not than anyone could do it. Fortitude is developed alongside of will. Anytime you feel you want to give up or give in keep in mind the next step can be taken but must be taken by you. The greatest successes in life were due to the person's ability to manifest fortitude in the face of adverse situations.

Stories of people like Helen Keller, Gandhi, Abraham Lincoln, Martin Luther King, Martin Luther, and many others demonstrate the power of perseverance in the face of dangerous and incalculable odds. The human spirit has many attributes. One of them is the ability to continue despite hardship. It is our resilience. You must tap into this portion of yourself in times of struggle.

6. Integrity:

"Adherence to a code of values;
incorruptibility"

Every person should have a code of values that keep them centered. This is their personal philosophy about life. This philosophy could be the result of philosophical studies, or it can be the sum of wisdom derived from life experience. You must have a solid perspective on things. This is important as it is the basis of your moral compass. What you consider to be right comes from this core of values. In life, you will be faced with many different scenarios that will test your integrity. This does not get easier the more successful you become.

In fact, the more successful you are the more challenging it is. Success brings with it a slew of temptations and trying situations. Success entails a greater level of achievement which brings with it riches, fame, and more responsibility. Having the integrity to do what is right in the face of temptation is mandatory. A strong sense of integrity is the key in developing and sustaining the flow of energy needed toward greater things in life.

The three-part definition means staying fixed in your core values and aligning these values with your goals so that each could support the other along your path. Never allow the ills and temptations of life corrupt you. Sometimes you may have to do things you don't want to do for you to get to where you want to be. This is the maxim of doing what you must do, for you to do what you want to do.

When we die, nothing we have accumulated in life such as wealth, skill-sets, or beliefs can be taken with us. From this point you can see you are more than your accomplishments and possessions in life. Whoever that may be is what goes with you at the time of your transition. This is who you must find during life. This is the essence of your-self.

It lacks for nothing and as such is complete. You must find this along the way. Having integrity will help you stay pure in heart, mind, and spirit as well as maintain a reasonable approach to life's hazards no matter the temptations that arise on your path. Think of having integrity as being stubborn in a good way.

7. Love:

The best of all has been saved for last. You may have noticed there is no dictionary definition presented here. This has been done intentionally. It was believed the meaning of love varies for everyone. It is only right you have your own concept of love and what it means to you. Love is powerful. No matter how that power is interpreted a truly valuable and meaningful experience can be derived from its presence in your life.

The feeling of love should be the motivating force of all your actions. Love is why we as a species exist. Love is the reason why the original creative force of this universe, whatever form or name you give that force, made the initial effort to create all that is and all that will be.

Love is the attractive force of all energies. It is the purest, highest expression of human sentiment, and divine compassion. Without love we would not have made it this far in our evolutionary process over the millennia. We would have destroyed our-selves long ago without it. Fraternity, Brotherhood, sisterhood, motherhood, fatherhood, family, friends, and even enemies are bound by love.

We create through love. We destroy through love. We live through love. We die through love. All this is possible as love is the purest rate of vibratory energy that exists in the universe. Love is the basis of motivation to create works like this. It is because of the love of humanity and creation that this text was created. Love is the only force powerful enough to lead humanity away from the path of decadence and destruction it is currently engaged in.

Loves power dictates you allow it to guide you every-day in every way. This is the only way to obtain the purest results from your actions. Each act done in the name of love will not only uplift you, but others around you. You are not alone in this world. You are connected to all that is. All that makes up the universe is within you: All in one, and one in all.

There are, at the time of this writing, 7 billion people in this world. Like it or not we will rise together toward progress or fall together in destruction. It is not only your success or failure that depends on love, but the success of humanity. Our success or failure on this planet depends upon how much of our actions and choices are guided and done in the name of love.

If the power of love, the binding attractive force that unites in positive and productive advancement, is used by a greater portion of the inhabitants on this planet, then the choices of those people will eliminate the negative circumstances experienced on this planet. It is only through this power can we end the madness that has overcome our minds and spirits, casting a spell that has us believing we are separate from each other.

Our fate depends on how much love governs our actions. Love yourself unconditionally and love all others unconditionally. Love this miracle of creation and respect it out of love. Do all with a sense of love. Understand Love is synonymous

with truth. Love can never go wrong.

7) Overcoming Self-destructive habits

-Aristotle

Sometimes the thing that prevents a person's success is them self. Oft times the obstacles you face in life are created by you. People tend to get in their own way. It's possible you've done something that made things harder for your-self. Life doesn't come with instructions and most people trod haphazardly along trying to figure things out through trial and error. The chances of making a mistake are increased in this process.

We only get one chance to do things right. Life is short and you cannot start over. One bad choice can lead to an avalanche of bad reactions. There are many self-destructive habits people engage in that prevent their success. The first of them is to think and believe you will fail at a project prior to, or during the process of fulfillment. Thinking you will fail at something is a surefire way of ensuring you will; the body follows the mind and if your mind doesn't believe, your body won't either.

You can if you think you can. Likewise, you can't if you think you can't. Even if you don't reach the point you wanted to get to, there is always value in the experience. Keep in mind you must eliminate all thoughts of failure. Don't defeat your-self before you try. When you think of failure your mind will believe it.

It will unconsciously send messages that will make it engage in acts that sabotage your projects. You ever find your-self in a situation you were close to accomplishing, and out of nowhere did something un-expected that ruins the whole thing? That's what I am talking about. You sabotage your-self. This must be stopped. Develop the habit of thinking the glass as being half-full.

Reality bites, and Positive thinking is believed to have no value. However, this is incorrect. Many great leaders and accomplished men and women all faced difficulties. What fueled these people was their ability to envision the desired end, their accomplishment of it, and the ability to continue even in the face of trying situations. Optimism is an asset.

Adopt the habit of being optimistic every day and every moment of your life no matter how trying the situation. Stop getting in your own way. Not only can your thoughts and feelings create a barrier to your success, but daily habits you believe are inconsequential. The first step to discovering bad habits or traits that keep you down is to make a list of them.

You must locate and identify parts of yourself that have been bad for you. These are character traits that are not doing you any good and must be eliminated. Once the bad traits are identified and their effect on your circumstances, you must begin to engage in a step by step process of gradual elimination of these faulty characteristics.

- The step by step process you can engage in to accomplish this can go as follows:

A. Find a quiet place to sit and write.

Gather some paper and a writing instrument

B. Draw a line down the middle of the page and across the top leaving a small piece of the center line protruding from the middle.

C. Write down the following on the left-hand side of the paper and the right hand respectively: Virtues and vices.

D. Write a list in the appropriate column of all the virtues you believe you have, and in the appropriate column all the vices you believe you have.

E. Be brutally honest with yourself. If you
need extra help in figuring out what parts
of you are beneficial and what are not ask
a close friend or relative. Moreover, in
more complex cases ask someone who
you know is not fond of you. They may
be more than obliged to let you know
about yourself. You may be surprised to
hear about what qualities you have both
known and unknown, good and bad.

F. Whatever the list of qualities written on
the virtue side of the list, work on making
those more prominent and stronger.
These are the habits and character traits
that have been helping you in life.

G. Whatever list of qualities are on the vice
side of the column are the ones you must

address. You must work on eliminating those from your character. The first step in doing so is to find the origin of those traits. Why did you begin them in the first place? Then you must analyze the impact they have been having on your life. Finally, you need to figure out how to eliminate them from your general character makeup. This requires a deep understanding of your-self and what you need to do to accomplish this. Some instances will require a simple adjustment in behavior. Others will require outside help.

- Work on bettering your-self by eliminating bad character traits and habits that have been holding you back in life. The following are a few suggested be reviewed first:

A. Your speech: How do you speak? Do you curse a lot, do you use slang? Do you speak clearly and pronounce all syllables, or do you slur your words? Clear speech is a must in proper character development and a good habit to develop. One of the things people gauge about you is how well you speak. Articulate speech is a sign of a sound and intelligent mind. Most people of a developed and noble character type will tend toward those they believe are of the same character. Your speech will reveal who you are.

B. Your gait and posture: How do you walk and stand? Do you walk with a bop? Do you stand straight, or do you slouch? Do you sit straight, or do you slump in your seat? Again, the mind and body are one, and how your body carries itself is a sign of how the mind carries itself. So, if you are constantly slouching and walking in an erratic fashion this is reflective of your thought patterns and how they function. Be mindful of your body language. It makes up at least 90% of all communication.

C. Your Eye contact and connection: When you interact with people do you make eye-contact, or do you avoid it? Do you pay close attention to what people say or do, or do you act like you're interested in something else? When you are engaging in social interactions with another you must be involved in that social interaction. The worst thing to do is speak to someone and not give them your full attention. Constant eye contact is an indication you are giving your full attention.

D. Your dress and fashion: Everyone has their own style of dress. Clothing is an outward expression of the personality and taste of a person. However, this clothing represents you and says a lot about you. So, understand your choice of fashion may not be acceptable in all circumstances. For instance, don't go to a job interview with ripped jeans and cutoff (unless the interview calls for it). The gist of this is to keep in mind how you dress, how it affects your environment, and the reactions of those within your environment.

E. Your Social Interactions: How you treat others is an indicator of your character, and poor treatment of others is a sign of a bad character. Be mindful of how you treat others. Remember the golden rule: Do unto others what you would like to have done to you. Likewise, the following is true: Don't do to others what you would not want to have done to you. So always be courteous and respectful towards others. If you are ever slighted by someone don't take it to heart, forgive and move on.

The development of good habits is crucial in this process. It's a part of developing a positive sense of self and taking responsibility for what that self does and creates. You are the builder of your life. Develop and build your character as well as your mind by generating good habits that will help to advance you along your path.

8) Overcoming failure and inner conflicts:

*"As a player you cannot lose, those who win
Carry off the fruit of their victory and yet
Those who are defeated have learnt valuable
Lessons that may turn the tide for tomorrow"*

-Author unknown

It is unknown for sure how many people have gone through life succeeding at every-thing they do, every time they do it, the first time they do it. For those who have had this experience I must say you are truly blessed, and truly wise, for only the wise and blessed could journey through life without fault or mistake.

For everyone else, including myself, who have had some trying times in life due to their own fault or through no known fault of their own; setbacks and failures are a part of life. Sometimes, even after trying, you don't succeed at what you set your sights on. Failure does exist and will be experienced some time or another in life. We are all human, and as such tend to fall under the spell of discouragement and depression after suffering some form of failure or shortcoming.

This experience can bring with it a sense of inadequacy and cause a complex or fear to develop. This complex could prevent you from ever trying to accomplish a goal again. At which point you could begin to lose even before you start for not even trying in the first place.

A result of this is the development of inner conflicts as you will begin to have issues with self-esteem and adopt bad habits to compensate; habits that have the potential to be destructive. The idea of Failure should not be considered a negative thing in every instance. If there is ever a time you don't succeed at something you set out to accomplish, don't become discouraged.

Take the time afterward to reflect on the situation. You must engage in a careful and accurate analysis to determine the cause of the failure. This is what is considered going back to the drawing board. It means to re-evaluate your plans and check for something you may have missed early on. No matter the cause the objective here is to learn from the experience, so you won't repeat it again.

Doing the same thing repeatedly expecting different results is insane. It is not failure that defines the context of the situation, what you have learned from it does. You must draw meaning from your experiences. All experience is not going to be positive. Some will be negative. Be aware of what each situation means. Assimilate what you learn from it and continue in life.

If you do not learn from your mistakes and failures, then you will be doomed to a life of repeated mistakes and failures. Repeating the same bad acts will always bring about the same bad effects. When you do learn from your failures you open for yourself a completely new world of opportunities and potential for success. The benefit of making a mistake is that now you know what not to do.

The next time you try to accomplish a goal you will operate from a point of experience and do exactly the right things to succeed. You will leave out anything you know will be harmful.

The odds of succeeding increase in your favor. The worst thing you can do is allow a failure or mistake deter you from your future goals. Avoid the habit of dwelling on past mistakes unless it is to analyze them. The past is to learn from, not dwell on.

It is dangerous to do otherwise as it creates a deeply embedded psychological wound and emotional complex. The subconscious complex could surface and cause you to do things to sabotage your plans or prevent you from even trying in the first place. Use past failures as a beacon to guide you in all steps you take from here on. Life is about forward motion.

The best part about evolution is that It always strives for perfection though it does not know what that perfection is. It just knows it must keep going. You are a part of that universal process. The process of evolution makes you want to be and do better. It is your universal right to live the best life you can. Experience the best of it you can despite the difficulties and adversity you come across along the way.

It is your choice as to how you want to live, and your responsibility to accept the consequences of those choices. Sometimes the choices lead to failure. It happens. The objective is to choose not to let it keep you down or repeat them. Utilize failure as a stepping stone that leads you closer to your next goal. This is how you overcome failure. You cannot change your past, but you can change your future.

<u>Part 4</u>

<u>CAVEATS</u>

"An individual's external reality

Is created by their

Internal reality"

\-   According to the
The laws of mind and Correspondence

I.   Mind states and feelings to avoid:

"The state of your life is nothing but a reflection of your state of mind"

-Dr. Wayne W. Dyer

You will not have unbridled control over each aspect of your external environment, nor over most circumstances you'll encounter along the way, but you do have the ability to control your actions in response. You always have control over how you act, or re-act in any given situation. You have control over how your environment influences you, and what part of it you will allow to do so. If you ever come across a stressful or difficult situation you can consciously control the mental, and emotional states you feel.

Always strive to keep from your mind any negative image or feeling that may try to overtake you. Do not repress the negative states when they rise. Allow them to pass, so you can continue to enjoy a better mental state. Constant equanimity and calm poise allow you to reach homeostatic balance. This creates an optimal state of performance ability.

In this state you can accomplish greater feats as the mind is able to function clearly, being free from the negative environmental stimuli that slow it down. It's like giving a car a tune-up every 3000 miles to maintain its performance. Your mind is the same way. Its functions depend on what you put into it. Like a car, or computer, the fuel or info you put into them may be harmful or helpful. The mind needs the best of everything to function properly.

Negative feelings and emotions slow the mind and body down. You must be mindful of what you expose yourself to and how you let it affect you. The more you avoid negative mind states and emotions in response to external stimuli, the greater the power you develop over how you act in response. This gives you the ability to continue to create with a clear and aware mind.

It will take an extraordinary amount of will and patience to do so. Humility is another quality you must adopt. You must adopt as there will be many times in life where you will find being humble is the best response. Lose the ego, humble yourself. Doors will open and you will need these qualities to reap the benefits. The following is a short list of top mindsets and feelings to avoid along your path.

Follow this list and discover what parts you have in you. Then begin the process of strengthening your-self mentally and physically to continue despite them. You will come across many more ill mind-states in your life, but from here on end you will be prepared to identify them, protect yourself from them, and act accordingly.

1. Laziness:

-     Proverbs 12:24

One of the worst Mind States you can have is laziness. Procrastination is the most prominent expression of this mindset. The reason laziness is so bad is that how will you ever get anything done when you don't do anything? Laziness and its partner procrastination are in complete opposition to effort and action. Remember that effort and action are key components to the process of living with creative intent, positive change, and evolution.

Effort and action are necessary to accomplish your goals and succeed in life. Laziness and procrastination will negate these qualities in an instance. Your progress will become stagnated keeping you un-productive and un-successful throughout life. It is easy to be lazy. It is easy to say you will do one thing or another at another time that never comes. Easy does not do it.

This does not entail all goals must be difficult to reach, but it does infer that a modicum of effort must be put into any endeavor to see it to its fruition. Procrastination will leave you in the same spot you started in. The lazy fail in life, and often become a burden upon the more industrial. Laziness can also lead you into a parasitical state where you find your sustenance in the efforts of others. You must avoid this form of dependence at all cost.

Life is not easy. It wasn't intended to be. Strength does not come from ease, but from difficulty. Resistance and hardship develop strength. Look at weight-lifting. The weights provide resistance to the weight-lifter when lifted. This resistance is difficult at first as the weightlifter may not be strong enough at that moment to adequately lift the weight. However, after constantly lifting the weight he or she begins to lift the weight more easily.

The muscles are forced to strengthen themselves to accomplish the task. The strength of the weightlifter is increased. He or she then begins the task of lifting heavier weight starting the process over again. Nature, in all her wisdom understands this. The creator knows it. It's just us who try to avoid and deny this truth. We want everything fast and easy.

We do everything in our power to avoid having to put in much effort. Instead, we put the effort into trying to circumvent it. Just think if everything in life were easy. Anything that a person would want to accomplish would be done so with the minimum amount of effort. The words Expert, Master, and Professional would no longer have any meaning, nor come with the acknowledgment and prestige they deserve. Life is diverse.

One of the most important laws of nature is diversity through evolution. Through the evolutionary process many forms of the potential end are present. Those that manage to last and survive continue to exist. All that do not, or are not capable of adapting, will cease to exist. New forms of life are then strengthened and molded through time until the best possible version is created.

Survival of the fit is the first and most un-avoidable natural law on this Earth. It ensures the lazy and un-productive forms of life on this planet do not make it into the next stage of life. Without this the lazy and un-productive would benefit from their unproductiveness as the necessary effort, action, will and strength it takes to reach the height of professionalism will not be needed.

This is contrary to natural law. Though our modern-day technology and social systems have been built to reduce the effects of this law, it still governs our overall existence. Be industrious. Continue to work toward your desired end and take the steps necessary to do so. Shun laziness

and procrastination at every turn.

2. Envy:

-    Jean Vanier

Envy is the painful or resentful awareness of another's advantages. When you envy, you spend an extraordinary amount of time desiring the goods and successes of others. When faced with the reality you do not have most of what you desire in life and another does, you may develop an antagonistic complex towards that person or persons. This takes away time and mental resources from your-self. Do not envy someone else. Instead of worrying about what the next person has, go out and get your own.

This is the essence of Creating with conscious intent. There is no room for envious feelings or thoughts. There will always be a time when you find someone else is in a better position than you are. This process is intended to give you the tools needed to get you where you want to be. There is no law saying you cannot obtain for your-self that of which someone else also possesses. Envy is a negative attitude you must avoid at all cost.

If you ever come across anyone who has what you want or is in the position you want to be in, do not envy that person. Instead, ask how that person got to where he or she is at. They may not expose all their secrets, but you may receive valuable information that can help you along the way. Each time you learn something from someone who is in a place you want to be it brings you that much closer to your goal.

You can do far more with learning how to get to where you want to be than you would by envying those already there. It follows an age-old maxim: Give a man a fish and he will eat for the day, teach a man to fish and he will eat for the rest of his life. Envying another person for their ability or possession is counterproductive towards this end.

You will spend more time thinking about what that individual has than you would on how to get your own. Moreover, envy is a negative mind-state which creates other issues for the mind and body. This will be discussed later. Shun envy in all its manifestations. To envy does not benefit and has no part in the life you are creating

for yourself.

3. Dishonesty:

*"He who permits himself to tell a lie once,
finds it much easier to do it the second
time."*

— Thomas Jefferson

Dishonesty is a big no-no in this process. In fact, it is a big no-no in life period. Remember the first part of all this requires that you be completely honest with yourself. The second part is to be honest with others as well. Being dishonest with others is akin to being dis-honest with yourself. If your actions are based on a lie, then all that follows those actions are a lie. Moreover, if the actions of others are based on a lie you told them, then you have robbed them of their right to act truthfully.

Imagine all you are doing right now is based on a lie someone had told you. How would you feel about that? It would call into question whether the current reality you are now living is the one you would be living had you not acted on the lie. When the action taken is based upon a lie the effects that come about are highly questionable. When a person addresses reality as it is, and not on a falsehood, the odds of succeeding increase.

The success gained is likely to last longer. Always be honest in all your dealings. If you can't be honest, then maybe it is not your dealing. The truth is not always pleasant. If it were meant to be it would not be the truth. Dishonesty with others is a negative way to deal with life. This approach is never beneficial.

The ultimate outcome of those who ensnare themselves into a web of lies is they get caught up in that web. It is incredibly difficult to get out of. By lying you put yourself into more trouble than that of which you sought to avoid when telling the lie in the first place. Do not be dishonest in any of your dealings with others.

4. Complacence:

"Complacency is the deadly enemy of spiritual progress; the contented soul is the stagnant soul"

- Aiden Wilson Tozer

Being satisfied with what you are, and where you are, is not a bad thing. It does not infer you are deficient in any way. Mind you, living with creative intent does not seek to improve you through the belief you are in-adequate or anything less than a beautiful human being. The idea of not being complacent with your current circumstances in life only seeks to pose the question of why stop here? This is not to say be ungrateful or unhappy with the blessing's life has given you. Always be grateful for your blessings.

The concept presents the premise that the drive necessary to compel you to move forward is derived from the dis-satisfaction felt at your present circumstances. It's consistent with the adage: 100% dis-satisfaction brings about 100% change. For you to get more from life, you must want more from life. You can keep what you have. You do not have to rid your-self of what makes you happy, but always strive for the best life has to offer.

Never be complacent. Life is so full of abundance and opportunity. If you choose to, you can begin to take the steps necessary toward taking part of that abundance that so many are already taking part in. The dis-proportionate division of wealth and resources among the peoples of this planet is not the normal or natural state of things.

The planet earth has more than enough to supply everyone with what they need, and most with what they want. The difference in the allocation of sources is dependent upon the amount of effort put into obtaining those sources. The secret to it all is in the industriousness of the individual. If you do not seek to obtain for yourself, then you will not obtain for yourself. Nothing is given. Everything is earned.

You must know this process is not an abracadabra way of producing all your hearts-desire with just a wishful feeling. This process is intended to instill within you the belief you create what you want in life, but through your effort and actions will you do so. Most important it is your responsibility to make it happen, as well as deal with whatever consequences that result from your choices.

If you possess the desire to improve your current situation, or even someone else's, then you must shun the feeling of complacence. You must act toward making things happen. Complacence is the cousin of laziness. Each has a positive reinforcement toward the other. Complacence is stagnation, and stagnation is death. By the end of this process you will be a conscious creator of your life, creating your life as you will it. This is the only way you will get to where you want to be.

5. Guilt:

"When you are guilty, it is not your sins you hate, but yourself"

- Anthony Demello

If you are reading this and can say with complete honesty you have never done anything in life for which you do not feel any guilt for, then you are truly a saint. For the rest of us where to err is a common occurrence, there is most likely something in our closet for which we may hold regret or a guilty feeling for having done or allowed to be done. Most people have done something this day which causes regret for tomorrow.

Despite the fact you may have felt, or still feel the pangs of regret and guilt, it is perfectly alright to forgive your-self and move on; in other circumstances to forgive others as well. To err is human. This present's the question of whether it is fair to allow our past actions to prevent us from future blessings and success. The answer is No. Everyone in life deserves a second chance.

However, you must give yourself that chance. The first step to doing so is to forgive your-self. You forgive yourself by understanding what happened in the past no longer exist. Continued self-punishment will not change anything. You may still feel some effects of what happened, or didn't happen, but the fact remains it no longer exists. Guilty feelings do not change what happened in the past.

They can change what will happen in your future. Feelings of guilt prevent you from doing or obtaining good as your feelings of guilt will lead you to believe you don't deserve it. This is a false and self-created mental block to the good life has to offer. The burden of guilt will interfere with your life and hold you back. It's like holding a ton of bricks that makes you suffer under its weight.

You must let that burden go. Sometimes this takes some deep reflection followed with an attempt to resolve whatever issue is causing the guilt. Sometimes you just must let go and accept things for what they are. Other times you should seek outside help. Whatever the remedy, it is you who must discern the best recourse that allows you to let go. Do not let guilty feelings hold you back in life. Forgive yourself. Allow yourself to move on without holding on to unnecessary emotional baggage.

6.   Negative Thoughts:

*"Be careful of what you think, your thoughts
run your life"*

-Proverbs 4:23

Thoughts are things. They exist as concrete, but abstract forms of reality. It seems paradoxical but makes perfect sense when understood. Thoughts are energy forms generated in our heads when we concentrate on a specific thing. They travel down axons and through dendrites crossing synaptic bulbs as bio-chemical neural transmitters. After developing in the cerebral cortex, they travel down the peripheral nervous system sending messages to all the different portions of our body.

Some of the messages are conscious, some are not. Though our thoughts can't physically be felt outside our own mind, the effects of those thoughts can be seen and felt through our actions. Every manmade creation, economic system, ideology, philosophy, and reality began in the mind of a human being. We are creators of mind by nature. We were designed that way.

It reflects an attribute of our creator. It's like your child having a characteristic you passed on to him or her. It can either be a gift or a curse depending on how you use it. That is a big issue with most of humanity. We were brought up being taught what to think, not how to think. The mind is your most valuable tool. Once you learn how to use it you will begin to make un-imaginable changes in your life.

What you must know about your mind is to stay away from negative thoughts. Your ability to create mentally corresponds with the original creator's ability to create. This is reflective of how the universe was formed. The universe reflects the thought of the creative universal mind. As such it follows that your creations will reflect the thoughts of your own mind.

Negative thoughts, speech, and feelings will create negative experiences. Your mind will subconsciously make you take actions to create the negativity you think. As such your reality will reflect the nature of the negative thought you formed. You will never enjoy the fruits of success, abundance, or love in life until you rid negative thoughts from your mind.

Success, abundance, and love are attributes that require the energy of a positive mind to obtain. If something positive is obtained through negative means it is taken back immediately through the re-action of the initial act itself. You are responsible for how you think and for the effect those thoughts generate. You must understand your mind is the first and foremost unit of creation in your life.

This is not a statement shrouded in mystical formula. It is a proven fact of basic human psychology. If the quality of the thought is of a positive and constructive nature, then the creations of that thought will be of a positive and constructive nature. What you want in life can be obtained. You can do so if you take the steps necessary to obtain it. The first step begins with a thought.

The second step is to understand the nature of the creation will follow the nature of the thought that created it. You want good things in life. You must have good thoughts. A key to conquering the temptation to fall into patterns of negative thinking is to practice its opposite: Optimism. Optimism exists for a reason. That reason is to cancel out negative thinking.

Use optimism everyday no matter the circumstances and it will not only get you past the circumstances but plant the seeds of better circumstances in your future. Refrain from all forms of negative thought. Again, your thoughts have an impact on your overall character and demeanor, as well as all actions you take. Adopt the notion the glass is half full, on its way to becoming full, and will flow over in abundance.

Do this on a regular basis until it becomes habitual. You will notice a change in your attitude toward certain situations that once gave you heartache and anguish. Now you will be able to deal with them in a calm and effective manner. You will also notice people will be more prone to address you in a kind manner as you will display an aura of positivity and strength in the face of adverse situations. You will become the pillar of strength people gravitate towards in times of hardship. Your thoughts also have a significant impact on your physical health as well.

7. Negative Feelings:

"Do not allow negative feelings and emotions to control your mind. Emotional harm does not come from others; it is conceived and developed within ourselves."

-    Carlos Slim

The recommendations to refrain from harboring negative feelings are based upon reasons akin to those for staying away from negative thoughts. However, the difference here is the negative feelings have more of an adverse impact upon your health. The human being is psychological as well as biological. The two are intertwined in a dance for homeostatic balance that allows the entire unit to function at its most optimal level.

The use of the mind in relation to the body can have a positive or negative effect on you.

Negative feelings such as anger, hate, malice, envy, jealousy, resentment, and many others bring about a constant state of stress and tension in the body. This upsets the bodies' normal homeostatic balance. The homeostatic balance in the body is disrupted as it is constantly forced to face the effects of this negative emotion by releasing bio-chemical secretions into the body to counter the effects of the emotion.

These hormones are released from various glands of the endocrine system into your bloodstream. The bio-chemical secretions, namely cortisol, adrenaline, epinephrine, norepinephrine, and others are used as defense mechanisms to help aid in coping with numerous stressors caused by experiences in life.

Nature has endowed us with natural chemicals in our body that help alleviate pain, anguish, and stress. It helps us prepare against adverse environmental circumstances. Our mental functions gather the information from the environmental stimuli through our senses. Our psychological makeup processes the information and decides the best course of action.

Our emotions are triggered by the information, which then triggers the appropriate glands of the endocrine system, bringing about the correct response to the stimuli. Our emotional makeup is the determining factor in how, when, and what chemicals are generated and released. The caveat is this: There does not have to be any external stimuli present to trigger the body's internal defense mechanisms.

Our emotional makeup can, at any given time (especially when the thoughts are of a negative nature), trigger these defense mechanisms even when there is no presence of an actual threat. The longer you stay in a negative emotional state, the longer the body produces and secretes the chemicals into your bloodstream.

The prolonged activation of the body's defense mechanisms through your negative emotional state saturates the bloodstream with bio-chemicals it does not need, nor can handle. Your body will begin to break down from the stress you have created and in fact begin a new process of trying to heal itself. The immune system is triggered and takes away much needed blood cells from an actual threat; leaving the body open to external threats that can cause true damage to the body.

Your negative feelings can make you sick through the unnecessary triggering of the body's defense mechanisms. It is important to ensure you're mental and emotional health is in a positive and calm state. Keep both your mind and heart free from negative emotional states. Life will bring you situations that can and will provoke a negative response. The object is to refrain from staying in this state for long.

Do not provoke these states with your thoughts and emotions when there is nothing going on to trigger the reaction. You not have to respond to an adverse situation in a negative manner. You can choose to act in response to a thing and choose how you want to act. This requires the development of Emotional Intelligence. The definition of Emotional Intelligence is the capacity to be aware of, control, and express one's emotions, and to handle interpersonal relationships judiciously and empathetically.

It is a powerful thing when you control your emotions. You must have control over your thoughts and emotions for you to have control over your body and life. You are responsible for developing this ability. This process will not teach you how for there are countless methods of doing so. You must do the research to determine what works best for you. Make the choice not to allow negative thoughts or feelings consume your daily state of being. Choose to act consciously upon your internal and external environments in such a way that allows you to

bring about the most optimal psycho-biological

states possible.

II. Types of People to avoid:

-Booker T. Washington

People are social beings. We must interact. All social projects, and the progress of those projects, depend upon the actions and cooperation of two or more people. One generates nothing. It takes two. Considering this you must be very careful in your dealings with others. The fact of reality is that everyone is not out for your best interest. Oft times it is those who are within your immediate circle who do the most damage. It can be anyone, even the most unexpected.

There is a saying in the Christian bible to the effect that bad associations spoil useful habits.

This means it does not matter how good your intentions are, if there are people around you who are of ill-intent then your project could be sabotaged, or worse: fail altogether. The following is a brief list of the types of people you should, and in some cases, must avoid at all cost.

Their presence in your life will most definitely interrupt the possibility of your goals becoming realized. It may lead to your complete ruin in extreme cases. The following list the main types of people to avoid. You can also develop, through your own discretion and insight, your own list. This will increase the chances of your projects being realized without some of the dangers from others that could affect you.

The Addict

The person with an addictive personality is one of the most dangerous types. For these people the main priority in life is that of which fuels their addiction. People who have addictions to drugs, gambling, alcohol, and others will by any means necessary do what it takes to satisfy the urge of that addiction.

They will engage in actions that are detrimental to others, including you if you allow yourself to fall victim to it. Even those close to them are at risk. In fact, those closest to them will be the first ones victimized. The closest ones are the easiest to get to. It would be wise to know all aspects of the company you keep. Avoid people with serious addictions, unless it is to help them in some positive way. Otherwise be very cautious.

The Taker

Is there someone in your life who continually takes from you? This person borrows money; ask for help, favors, property, and other things on a regular basis without ever giving anything in return. If there is someone like this in your life that's draining you of your time and resources, then you must begin to distance yourself from that person.

They may be using you. Sometimes they do so intentionally, sometimes they do not. The focus is to comprehend the fact you are making your life and creating for yourself. Now, it is not wrong to give to others. To help one in need is a spiritual attribute and everyone should practice this. However, to aid one who is of ill intent towards you and seeks to get over, or one who refuses to help them-self due to laziness, or indolence is a fault. Helping hands are good, but tied hands are not. To enable someone in their faulty ways is a sin

There is nothing wrong with altruism. Our society exists through the work of humanity in common. The universal drive to benefit ourselves is fueled by the law that says it can only be done through the cooperation of others as well. It is essential we help one another. However, too much aid to someone can hurt both the giver and the receiver. In this instance the giver suffers a substantial loss of time, energy, and finance where the taker becomes highly dependent on the giver and thus incapable of ever being able to care for them-self. Be mindful of those who take too much and give very little.

The Irresponsible

Avoid those who have no sense of duty, commitment, or who refuse to accept any responsibility for their actions. How can you advance around those who are constantly engaging in irresponsible behavior that can harm you? The irresponsible do not advance far in life. Life only endows those who are responsible enough to navigate through the more complex aspects of life with the great amount of benefits it produces. Remember: You are now living with creative intent. This process is geared toward giving you the tools you need to construct your life the way you want it. Do not diminish your chances of success by surrounding yourself with those who are of the opposite nature.

The Fake Friend

Friends are a great blessing in life. They are on a level with family and are oft times mentioned along with them in conversation. A good friend is, in fact, family. However, the company of a bad friend can be a great bane to you. Sometimes it is difficult to discern the real from the fake. However, there are methods you can use to discover the true nature of your comrade.

Observe your friend, or friends. Ask yourself: does my friend treat me with respect and dignity? Does he or she always ask for things, and tells you no whenever you ask? Do they help you in your time of need, or do they abandon you? Are they always honest or lie? If they ask for something and you say no, do they become upset and distant?

The above are some telltale signs of ill intent. You can ask many other questions you feel will help you know who you have befriended. These are some basic questions intended to get you to analyze your relationships more closely. You can develop more after you experience the recurrence of certain scenarios in your life. The overall point in the matter is to be able to discern the real friends around you from the fake ones and separate the two.

It is like planting a pretty garden and then taking the weeds out after they grow. Know that first impressions are meaningless. A person will don any mask it takes to gain your acceptance in the first encounter. It is only through longstanding observation that their true intents can be discovered. A person putting up a false persona cannot maintain that falsehood constantly.

Eventually their true nature will show. You must know who you have befriended. It is those closest to you that can do the most harm. Friends are the second closest to you after family, and sometimes come before family. If you have discovered in some way that your friend is a bad one, then you must begin to distance yourself from that person.

People with bad luck and the fool

Avoiding people with bad luck is self-explanatory. Do not let their bad luck become yours. If someone is foolish in their ways, stay clear from them. Life has a way of protecting the child and the fool. Nature knows neither has the capability of fully understanding the effects their actions bring about, so they are held less accountable.

You, however, are fully aware of what you are doing. As a result, you are held fully responsible for your actions by nature. If you are with a foolish person, and that foolish person does something foolish, you will most likely pay the penalty. Do not put yourself in a position where you will suffer the consequences of a fool's behavior.

The Criminal

If you are not engaging in criminal behavior, then do not associate with those who are. If they go down you will go down with them, or for them. The criminal minded only care about obtaining the maximum amount of benefit with the minimal amount of loss. Don't think a criminal won't allow you to suffer the penalty for their actions. They will. Stay away from those involved with criminal behavior.

It was recommended you avoid certain mind and emotional states. It is also highly recommended you avoid those who engage in the mind states and emotions you avoid. If you are highly positive and energetic, do not surround yourself with one who is negative and lethargic. If you do you run the possibility of being drained of your energy by that person, and possibly becoming infected yourself with that person's negative energy.

It's akin to the saying that Misery loves company. Protect your mental and emotional well-being from both internal and external influences. There are many personality types that are wholly unconducive to your growth and development in life.

For your safety and well-being, you must avoid people with character types opposite of, and antagonistic toward that of your own. Mind you this should not act to condemn all those who are of a negative disposition. It simply means to be mindful of their possible impact on you and deciding on the best course of action in response.

Human beings are by their very nature good. However, this good must be nurtured and developed to become a strong and prominent characteristic of that person. The negativity of a person comes from the accumulation of experiences that have led the person to the negative side of the pole. The realities of life have either corrupted the person or made them bitter.

Some can pull out of this state. Some cannot. Those who have not may still be helped if the desire is there.

Those who are of a positive nature have the responsibility of attempting to aid those who truly desire to engage in a more positive path. Nevertheless, if those of a negative disposition cannot be helped, continue in your path and leave them behind. This is the meaning of Let the dead bury the dead.

Part 5

Self-Modification

"It is not as much about who you used to be, as it is about who you choose to be."

\-   Sanhita Baruah

I.   Re-inventing yourself:

Re-inventing yourself begins with understanding that who you were, or are, is not who you have to be. You can change, if you want to. The decision must be made by you, and it must be based on truth. The first step in this process is in knowing who you are, and how you became that person. Next, you must determine what changes are needed. Finally, act. Follow the plan set and make it happen.

Albert Einstein once said the definition of insanity is to continue to do the same thing repeatedly, expecting different results. If there are behaviors that lead to certain bad effects in your life you must change them. If you do not change what you do, then what you experience will remain the same.

If there are recurring bad events in your life, then the cause is within you. This cause must be discovered, worked on, and resolved so the effects can be changed. Understand all change must begin with addressing the cause. The prime cause of our behavior and experiences lies within the mind. Modify your thought behaviors, as stated prior, to a more positive and rational mindset. Take control of your emotions. Be an actor in life.

This means act in response to a situation, maintain control of yourself, and lead it towards the outcome you desire. This is how you create your life, by re-inventing yourself into the person needed to bring about the outcome you want.

Everything is in constant change throughout this world and throughout the universe. Evolution is a law of reality.

At each step of the process of unfoldment and change a part of what is unnecessary is left behind in lieu of what is conducive to growth. You are a part of that. If you are unable to work on yourself and change, then you will be left behind. You must follow the flow of progress. This flow consists of self-modification at each phase. Envision yourself as who you want to be.

Imagine the perfect version of you and be that. Picture your life as you want it to be. Act as if it already is. Think as the person you want to become thinks. Speak as that person speaks. Look like that person looks and surround yourself with the people that person would be around. Place yourself in the environments that support your character. It is self-transformation from the inside and out.

Continually follow the process of self-modification. Change your internal world and perception opening yourself up to newer forms of reality. In due time, you will notice you are a different version of your-self. Your external world will reflect this. Your world will be the shape in which you have made it and you will have become the perfect fit for it. This is not magic.

It is just a simple step in the process of change, progress, and unfoldment that occurs as a result of living with creative intent. Re-inventing yourself will open the door to numerous possibilities for success and advancement. You will be able to handle more that life has to offer, because you can fit the role needed for it. You will naturally gravitate towards, and attract to you, that of which is necessary for your success. This is process of creating your life.

II. Overcoming fear of change:

"Change is inevitable, Growth is optional"
-Anon

People are afraid of change. The thought of the unknown can bring on a sense of fear. Change is often a source of anxiety and inquietude. As a result, change is not worked toward. This is a self-imposed obstacle based upon a thought of fear in your mind. This barrier is always present when a decision must be made whether to change, or not. You know what you have, don't know what you will get, and may be unwilling to take a risk. Familiarity brings with it a sense of comfort. Change can be, and often is, a threat to that comfort zone.

However, the fact is the biggest events in your life are the result of some form of change. The greatest constant in life is change. Do not fight it. Change will happen no matter how hard you fight. Adapt to the changes that happen and allow them to let you become a better person. Treat each experience of change in your life as a breath of fresh air. You will most definitely experience great changes in your life after reading this book.

These changes are ones you are consciously bringing about, so don't be afraid of it when it does. During the times you feel fear of an unknown future take a breath and find the strength to act despite that fear. Believe in yourself and know you will accomplish what you set out to do. No matter what all will always be well.

III. Being Realistic:

"I always like to look on the optimistic side of life, but I am realistic enough to know that life is a complex matter"

-Walt Disney

Aspiring toward becoming a better version of yourself, and enjoying the best life has to offer is a desire felt by many. No one wants a bad life of suffering and pain. It is a natural right for all human beings to have the chance to be happy. However, this desire must align with the level of your ability to accomplish it. This means do not try doing something you cannot possibly do. For example, if you are blind, then it would not be wise to try and be a pilot. During this process you must know yourself.

You must know who you are, and what you're reasonably capable of. Know your strengths and weaknesses. Know what areas you need to develop. This stage of the process requires a deep introspective analysis of yourself to determine whether you can accomplish the goals you have set for yourself. Your physical and mental health must be evaluated.

Moreover, you must be honest with yourself about the fact that you may have to incorporate new skills and characteristics to advance, as well as rid yourself of old characteristics that are unconducive to your growth and development. Being realistic entails looking at everything about yourself and current situation. Then you need to determine, based upon the results, the most practical and realistic road you can take.

When being realistic about the changes you desire in your life, and the initial impulse to act upon those desires, honesty with yourself is the firmest platform to stand on. It is from this realistic platform of self-awareness that you will begin a journey of self-modification, and do so successfully, as it will be based on accuracy and truth.

Part 6

Objective Application

"Knowing is not enough; we must apply.

Willing is not enough; we must do"

\-   Bruce Lee

I.   Setting Goals:

Setting goals was spoken of in part two. Now you will be shown exactly how to set goals. You will be provided with a process that will allow you to create the most effective way possible to achieve your goals. This will bring about the most maximum of results.

I

<u>Short term goals</u>

Short-term goals are goals that need to be accomplished within a short period of time. Usually this is within the week or month that you are still in.

The first step in this process is to get a small note pad, or notebook to be used for the sole purpose of writing your short terms goals list down. I personally use post-it notes, but you can utilize any writing material you feel comfortable with.

On the top of the paper write down "To do list for:" and then write the designated date of accomplishment next to it. Begin with a sequentially numbered list of items from the most important to the least. This is so you can see what your priorities are. It is always good to set the high priority goals at the top of the list so those can be done first.

Organize your schedule in such a way that allows you time to accomplish the goals you have set out for yourself. Try to follow the order you created. It is ok if you don't, but just keep in mind the ones at the top of the list are the ones that should be done first.

As you achieve each goal mark them off. This way you can keep track of what has been done. Always keep in mind the entire list must be achieved by the date you have set for yourself. Not only is this important to ensure you accomplish all you set out to do, but to develop a sense of discipline in keeping to the deadlines you have set for yourself. You must do what you say you are going to do in the time you say you will do it.

If in the event you are unable to meet the deadline for some reason simply place it at the top of the next to do list as the priority of that list. Do this until all the goals you have set for yourself are completed. Eventually this process

will become habitual and you will find yourself
completing all tasks you set for yourself with
ease. An example of a to-do list looks like this:

To do list for March 3/15-3/21:

1. Pay the rent
2. Clean the house
3. Wash the clothes
4. Go to PTA meeting
5. Pick up clothes at cleaners

<u>**II**</u>

<u>Long Term Goals:</u>

Long-term goals are, by their very nature, akin to short term goals but for one thing: They require an extraordinary amount of effort and energy to complete. This is so because of the amount of time the goal needs to come to fruition. Long term goals are goals that take a longer amount of time to complete. You must know what you want, know how to get it, and go for it. This is a straightforward plan of action but requires an amount of strength great enough to follow the plan over a long period of time.

You derive the strength necessary by applying the meaning of the words to know from part three of this program.

You are going to need all the strength you can muster to accomplish your long-term goals. It is during this process you will encounter numerous obstacles and possible setbacks. When something takes a long time to accomplish the likelihood of external forces intervening in an adverse way increase. Moreover, you need to have a great degree of patience.

The fact of the matter is that you are not going to see the fruits of your labors immediately. Long term goals can be likened to gardening. The initial step to gardening is to till the soil to ensure it is arable enough to plant in. Then you plant your seeds. Afterward you must constantly tend your garden and fend off weeds, insects, and protect your plants from the elements long enough to derive the fruits of your efforts.

Furthermore, just like having to know how to garden in the first place, do the research to gather the information you need to know to accomplish your goal. You then must make sure it is something you can accomplish and execute the plan. Finally, be diligent in maintaining the efforts and protecting your interest against outside forces that thwart your plans. In the end reap the fruits of your labor.

Always keep in mind the greater the goal, the longer it is going to take to accomplish. Do not let this fact deter you in any way. Anything great that is worth having takes' time to achieve. The phrase easy come easy go is not without a degree of truth. The last thing you want to see is the fruits of your hard-earned work leaving your grasp as soon as you get it. Follow the step by step process you have set for yourself.

Set a pace. Do not rush. Mark off each step accomplished in the same manner you would in the short-term goals. Overall, the most important thing to realize is you must continue until the very end of the project. Do not stop until you have succeeded.

II. Recording Progress:

Another part of the objective application of living with Creative intent is to keep track of the progress you make. It is suggested you keep track of all your progress and results in a journal or diary. Keep a daily record of your experiences, plans, thoughts, and progress. Look back to what you have written and done to make necessary adjustments. Ensure you are following the track you have set for yourself.

Analyze your actions and re-actions. Ask your-self questions in response. Are you following your own schedule? Do you notice any patterns of behavior or events? If so, is it bringing about positive or negative results? This is the time to really go over what you are doing. It is akin to balancing your check book, except it is the account of your life.

At this stage it is crucial you begin to record and analyze yourself and your life to determine if it is going in the trajectory you intend for yourself. This is called self-analysis. Self-analysis is essential as it is the only way to ascertain whether you are truly making progress or not. You may get feedback from people telling you of certain noticeable changes. However, you yourself must be able to determine what changes and advancements you have made.

Plan your daily, monthly and yearly schedule, and goals. Write down any and all information you need to accomplish your goals. Write down all information you believe is beneficial to you in some way either financially, spiritually, or personally. It is in the act of recording progress where you will find out the most about yourself as it will be a self-created reference point you can always look at.

Remember to always be honest in your writings. Honesty is the only policy when it comes to your-self. The only way you will receive an accurate reflection of your advancements is by recording an accurate account of those advancements. The same is true with any setbacks you encounter. Record these as well so you always have a reference point in case of failure. This way you can trace the root cause of it.

Recording your progress acts as the foundation of all your creations. It is your playbook. Your creations will only be as strong and accurate as the plans that have been followed to create them. Finally, use the book to write down any ideas you may come up with along the way. One of the worst things to believe is that you will always remember the genius idea that springs to you in a moment of clarity.

Write it down. Keep a record of all you do. It is the mature and responsible way to conduct your-self. You have control over your life, and part of that control derives from the ability to take note of the stages you go through so you can measure the change. Recording your progress is key. Make sure you are doing so. Otherwise most evidence of your work could be lost, or worse you can lose track of where you are going for failure to keep mind of where you are going.

III.   Networking:

While it is true this process emphasizes independence for your growth and advancement, you cannot make it happen alone. One creates nothing. It takes two or more to make a thing occur. Networking is an invaluable tool to develop and use. In fact, networking with other people is your greatest asset and necessary as a part of the process of making your plans become a reality.

Networking consists of getting out and meeting people. Now this isn't entirely for social purposes. This form of networking consists of making the right contacts in the right areas that will help you advance along your path. Do not think of this as a form of using people. This is far from it.

Not only are we responsible for ourselves, but we are responsible for others. The same is likewise true concerning you. Others are responsible for your well-being and advancement as well. Society exists upon the foundation of engaging in work for the common benefit and interest. So, I may do something with the aim of advancing along my own path, but help others along the way, or at the end.

Altruism is the glue that binds us all. The irony of it all is that altruism is based upon selfishness. We all help each other for the core fact of ensuring that our chances of survival are increased. We are only as strong as the least of our own, and the act of helping to build ourselves up as well as others is a humane one consistent with the advancement of humanity. So, for you to receive help, you must also be willing to give it.

If you are an extrovert this should not be a problem. If you are an introvert, then you must fight against you own natural inclination to stay to yourself and go out and meet new people. No matter your personality trait, whatever your goal in life, be it big or small, you will always find someone who is willing to give a helping hand.

People are good by nature. It is the failure to follow the natural law of unity, harmony, and peace amongst our species that creates the division between us. People have a natural inclination to help others. It is the distrust that has been created which prevents most people from doing so. Whatever the situation is always

network with others and remember this fact: one

hand washes the other and both wash the face.

IV.   Research:

Knowing what you want and setting goals are only parts of the overall process. You must also know as much as there is to know about the thing you set out to create. This is where good old-fashioned research comes in. With today's technology you can find out how to do just about anything. Set aside time to find out how to put into action what you have planned.

It is a simple concept but requires a lot of effort on your part. Always know that benefits are available in all types of research. You never know what valuable information you may come across. Whether it is what you intended to find or not. Research is a valuable tool that increases the likelihood of success.

Knowledge is the true source of wealth, and the more you know about how to accomplish the thing you set out to do, the greater your chances are at succeeding at it. The well informed always have an advantage over those who aren't. Success loves preparation, so prepare yourself by knowing and comprehending the process involved in achieving your goals.

If you take a moment and think about it, all educational and training institutions are research centers. The overall intent is to train the students to become professionally efficient at the trade or career they set out on. This increases the chance of success in the career field for the students who attended. It is the same concept here except for one thing: You are not being taught by another how to succeed at what you want to do. You are

teaching yourself.

V.   Self-Evaluation:

After learning and utilizing all you have seen in this process, especially in part 6, take the time to sit back and reflect on your works. You have been shown how to Set goals, network, research, and keep track of your progress. Now it is time for you to view the picture. Look at yourself in relation to the path you have walked so far. Who are you now compared to who you were?

Mark down the differences in your personal growth. This is the process of self-evaluation. Self-evaluation consists of looking back at your life from the point where you began and compare it to how you have developed since then. Self-evaluation is introspection. It is an absolute must that you take a moment and check yourself out.

The one thing in this world that everyone should have a basic knowledge of is themselves. Know you. Know who you are and who you aren't. Know who you want to be. Know the difference in who you were and who you are. The ancient Greek philosopher Socrates made the importance of this clear in this simple statement: "Know Thyself".

Knowing your-self gives you greater power over your-self and your life. Take a moment to look at all that has happened. This is to ensure you are still on the right path to your victories and success. It will ensure you are satisfied with the results as well. Take a minute to reflect. When finished, turn the page and get ready for the final part of the operative portion of living with creative intent.

<u>Part 7</u>

<u>Moral Responsibilities</u>

Destiny is a predetermined course of events

To the future.

Fate is the consequence of right or wrong

decisions.

The former cannot be predicted,

The latter can be foreseen.

I. Personal Responsibility:

"The moment you take responsibility for everything in your life is the moment you can change anything in your life"

-   Hal Elrod

There are four Pillars of personal responsibility to abide by when creating your life. They are Self-discipline, structure, rights and duties, and sacrifice. These are four attributes you must comprehend and incorporate into yourself as a requirement of living with creative intent. This will help you use the power you develop in a just way. Each will be studied in its own order. The first is Self-discipline.

<u>Self-discipline</u>

It is a cardinal rule of modern society that others must control those who cannot control themselves. The rationale behind this is that the person who lacks self-control bears within them the seeds of their own destruction and the destruction of those around them. Therefore, prison exist. Though the prison system does have its alternative methods of function, the main purpose of its existence does fulfill a social need. That is to keep society protected from those who seek to destroy it through deviant means. These deviant means mainly derive from the inability of an individual to control him-self. If you cannot control your-self through the lack of self-imposed discipline, then there is a system in place that will control you for you.

Self-discipline is the motivating force you will need to make your way in life and protect you from outside influences who seek to control you. Through the practice of a method of self-control you will allow the powers of focus, will, motivation, dedication, and enthusiasm to develop. These are strengths that will help you maintain control over your life.

Controlling your-self entails the control of your mental and physical functions to the point where your body is under the full control of your mind, and your mind is under the full control of itself by being aware. At this point you must be mindful to discipline your thoughts to prevent your mind from creating negative thoughts. Negative thoughts are a waste of mental energy.

Discipline your speech so that you may not say anything that is offensive or hurtful toward another, or your-self. There is power in the spoken word. The tongue is a double-edged sword, and its use or misuse can determine your fate in life. Be mindful of your speech. Discipline your actions so that you may not engage in any acts today that will be cause for regret tomorrow.

Discipline you're eating habits, so that what you eat will be cause for life and health, not sickness or death. Eat to live, do not live to eat. Discipline your waste habit's, our planet is not a garbage bin. Be mindful the things we use are from this earth and go back into it. Discipline your consumption habits. Just because it exists does not mean you must have it or consume it.

One of the most harmful parts of our current reality is the emphasis on materialism as our main ideology. There is much more to life than just having things. If you were to take a moment to think about this you will see this concept describes the reaping of vast sources of the earth and the fashioning of these sources into useable, and profitable goods. How much you want determines how much is produced.

How much produced determines how much is taken from the planet. Discipline your spending habits so you will not waste money on unnecessary items. Differentiate the wants from the needs. It is your responsibility to control yourself in all acts and endeavors. Just like the pilot of the plane controls the direction of the plane, your mind must be the pilot of your actions. You heart must be the co-pilot.

All acts and thoughts must be based on a balanced level between the two. Once you have mastered yourself and have full and conscious control over your mind and emotions, you can begin to exercise mastery over your-self and then your life.

Structure

Structure is a framework to follow from point A to point B. When applying structure to your life you will create for yourself a guide that takes you from start to end. You can begin to Structure your life through goal setting, as has been discussed in previous parts. Another way to create and develop structure in your life is to make a daily schedule. If there is anything you need to have structure in, it is in your daily life.

One of the biggest complaints made is that there is not enough time to do things. This is not true. There is always time to do something. The issue lies in the fact you have not organized your time efficiently enough to accomplish what you set out to do. Everything involves time, and if you were to organize your time you would be able to accomplish more.

You may have difficulty accomplishing a goal or task for the simple reason that you have not allocated the time it takes to accomplish the task. You must set aside time for the sole purpose of completing the things you need to get done. Live wisely by making good use of your time. All that exist does so within the framework of time. Time exists for the sole purpose of measuring and observing change.

Structuring your daily life ensures you have time for all the things you need to get done, and acts as a self-discipline that will allow you develop a greater sense of self-control. It is your responsibility to organize your life to ensure the best possible outcome. Create for yourself a structured way of living.

<u>Rights and duties</u>

Every living being bears rights in life from animals, to plants, to human beings, and even the earth itself. The universe has an inalienable right to exist. This existence has the right to evolve and express itself to the fullest of its nature and purpose. All that exist does so within the universal matrix of positive conscious love energy.

This means that everything created was done so with love and is held together by love. The failure to understand this and the violation of the laws set by this love are the cause of what is called sin. It must be known that for every right their lie's a duty not to violate that right. A violation of the right entails the misuse, misapplication, and/or violation of the law that governs the thing of which you are addressing.

As a human being you have a right to be free from aggression and violence from another. Any aggressive act toward you would be a violation of that right. You also have a duty not to violate the rights of others through aggressive acts, or any other form of violating behavior. If you keep in mind your responsibility to abide by your duty not to violate the rights of others, you will be able to avoid creating problems for yourself.

You are also responsible for asserting your rights. When necessary you must also let others know you have rights and assert those rights in instances when your rights may be violated. This is not an easy task and requires delicate attention for the definition of what is considered a right is interpreted in many ways by many people. Just know that if it feels wrong it probably is. Your intuition is always correct. Trust it. Recognize the rights of others and know your duty to respect those rights.

Sacrifice

"Non-Gratis". This is a Latin maxim that means Nothing in life is free. The concept of free is an illusion. Whenever something is given, something is taken from the source of what is given. There after lies a void in the place where the thing was taken, and time will tell if it is fulfilled again. If not, an imbalance occurs, and disharmony results.

With this fact in mind, the question must be asked is what are you willing to sacrifice and what price are you willing to pay for it? The gist of this is that you must be willing to give something up in the now, for you to reap the benefits in the future. The sacrifice does not have to be anything extraordinary or beyond your ability to give up.

You must be willing to sacrifice something in the now that is either preventing you from advancing, or the equivalent of what you desire. The measure of the sacrifice now must be the equivalent of what you desire in the future. For instance, if you have trouble breathing due to smoking, you must give up smoking now to obtain the ability to breath better in the future.

Another example is if a person is in a bad relationship and wants a better one. That person must sacrifice the current relationship to open the doors to a better one. These are just two examples of the sacrifice of something that is preventing you from obtaining more for your life in the future. The next form of sacrifice entails the sacrifice of something equivalent to that of which is desired.

For instance, in the musical profession it is said a person is a master or professional after having completed at least 10,000 hours of practice and playing. In order to reach this level 10,000 hour of that person's life must be sacrificed in dedication to the task. The sacrifice of this time now to become a master of the craft later is an equivalent sacrifice. A second example relates to the most prevalent form of exchange in our system: Commercial activity.

For every material item or service desired, a person must exchange an amount of money equivalent to the value of the good or service desired. How much money you are willing to spend or do spend determines what you get and how badly you want it. There is a price for everything in life. Nothing is free, and if you ever think you have received something for free understand the cost was paid even if it was not by you.

Sacrifice is a fundamental element of creative intent. You are responsible for making the necessary sacrifices for what you want. The sacrifice can be a material item, a mindset, or a habit. Whatever you do to accomplish your goals in life do so with an understanding that something must be given in return. There is no wrong in this.

Just know that if all you do and have is fully paid for in the eyes of society and nature you will owe nothing. In this state, you will have truly earned all that you have through your work, efforts, and merit.

II. Social Responsibility:

We do not live alone in this world, and your presence among others mandates a level of responsibility to others. Our society functions with the cooperation and mutual respect of all involved. Remember, we do not make things happen alone. It is a group effort. However, there are times that some members of our society need a little more help than others. This is OK. All human beings are created equal. Yet, as time goes on all do not remain equal. Some advance more than others.

It is the responsibility of those who can aid others to do so as they have the power to do so. The more you progress in learning how to create your life, the more social responsibilities you will have. The reason for this is that you will be able to make decisions that can affect the greater part of our society. We are as strong as our weakest link. To help others in need is an investment in strengthening our future. We are our brother's keeper.

(1) <u>Our responsibility to the poor-</u>

Our economic system is a fluid one which evolves over time to ensure its survival and continued functioning. One of the main effects of it is the natural, and sometimes un-natural, stratification of our society into various classes with the lines draw along the accumulation of wealth.

In this system, some people will thrive and become very wealthy. Others will lead a life of financial stability, and relative comfort. But others, and what appears to be much of the population, will find themselves in a class where money is not easily accessible and resources scarce.

The fact there exists people who do not have adequate financial means does not mean they are any less a part of our society. Moreover, it does not mean that those who do have and are well off are absolved of the responsibility to give aid to those who may need it. One of the most prevalent ills that plague our society is the disparity between the classes of people along economic lines.

It is a fact most of the wealth is in the hands and control of a small part of the population, and the majority are living in poverty. This does not mean those who are wealthy are evil in any way. Please understand that most people who are wealthy have earned that wealth through their own hard work and labor. Their efforts have allowed them to generate a great deal of wealth. That is one of the goals in this process: to give you the strength and means to succeed financially as well as personally.

Understand that most people who do not have a vast sum of wealth do not have it due to their own inability to put the necessary effort required to obtain that wealth. The point that must be understood here is that regardless of who has, and who doesn't, is the fact those who have are more responsible for the advancement of our society.

The reason for this is that those who are wealthy have the power to make great changes. If you can give aid to those who are in need it is your responsibility to do so. We are only as strong as the weakest among us. To help one in need is the equivalent of investing in our future by helping to lift and build up someone who may someday give a great contribution to our society.

Many great leaders and successful individuals have come from poverty. All people have the potential to add something positive to the human species. To marginalize those who do not have simply because they do not have is a moral fault. When you find yourself succeeding and becoming wealthier because of your efforts always remember your responsibility in giving aid to those who may be in a position you were once in.

Keep in mind this important statement: give aid to those who are in need and are attempting to improve their circumstances; be mindful of aiding those who do not seek to improve their circumstance, but merely want to find a host to live off. You will be harmed as you will be drained of your time and energy, and the one helped will only be enabled by your support.

(2) Our responsibility to the sick:

Humanity has been struggling with natures' elements with all her plague and beauty for millennia. One of the biggest of her attributes is disease. At one point, or another human beings have faced mass plagues of disease and virus. This is something we all fight together whether one suffers from something or knows someone who is. Despite one's personal health status the responsibility to give aid to one in need doesn't end.

Even if you're not a professional medical worker you still can help in other ways. Along with the infirm are the physically handicapped. Though our bodies are created to perform all necessary functions for survival, there are times that injury or some sort of genetic malfunction reduces an individual's ability to carry out normal task. If you come across a person in this state who needs aid, offer a helping hand.

(3) Our responsibility to the weak:

It may be that we are all born equal, but it does not always stay that way. At some point of time a person becomes different from another and develops attributes that give him, or her, an advantage in life. These qualities make one strong; and place them in a position of power. Those in positions of power have a greater responsibility in those positions so as not to abuse their power. Just because one is in a position of power does not call for the abuse of that position against those that are weaker.

(4) Our responsibility to the old:

Eastern societies have adopted a code of reverence for their elders as a social norm. They understand the importance of their elders. They are the people who paved the way to our present day from generations back. We stand on the shoulders of those who have come before us and should find meaning in the accomplishments they made and honor them for it.

Our duty is to create new and better ways of living to help guide future generations as did those who came before us. One of those ways is to set an example of how to treat the elderly. One day you will find your-self old and unable to perform task you may have when you were younger.

Treat the elderly the way you would want someone younger to treat you when you become elderly, because the fact of the matter is that everyone who lives will go through the aging process and be in the position most aged persons are in now. This includes you.

(5) Our Responsibility to the young:

In juxtaposition to our responsibility for the elder part of our society, we must also keep in mind the younger part. Their minds are still developing. They get most of their information and guidance from those who are older than them. Our influence as adults on the youth is great.

Therefore, it is a great responsibility as adults to ensure the youth of our society are steered toward a positive direction and are given a good example by us. They are the future of our society and our society will become what we impress on the youth today. The age-old adage it takes a village to raise a child still rings true in our modern-day society. We are all responsible for each other. Be a positive influence on the youth whether they be your own or not.

(6) Our responsibility to our society:

Indigenous Natives to this land embedded within their social consciousness the understanding that the interest of the tribe comes before any self-interest. They held this concept from childhood to old age. The interest of the whole tribe was the most important thing. Their very survival depended on it.

We all exist and function together within this social web, because all our actions within this web are geared towards it support and continued function. Even when we continue down a path towards our own self-interest we still help to contribute toward the interest of the social network, if what we are doing is contributing something positive.

We are in this together. Our survival depends on how well we work together. Remember this phrase: One in all, and all in one. The state of the world we live in is the result of the choices and actions made by humanity in the aggregate. So, let's do our best to ensure that our society both local, and worldwide does well heading forward

into the future. Think globally, act locally.

III.   Global Responsibility:

(1) Our responsibility to our immediate environment:

Our surroundings have a great influence over us in our everyday lives. The more suitable the environment the greater the likelihood it will have a positive impact on our mood and ability to function. Our households, our communities, and even the cities and towns we live in should always be kept in the best condition possible. The upkeep of the environment is the responsibility of those who inhabit it.

Always ensure you do your part to keep clean, safe, and positive your surroundings. Your home should be kept neat and clean. Your neighborhood should be free from litter, graffiti, loud noise and foul odors. The greater city or town you live in should be maintained and suitable for optimal social life and activity. This is the responsibility of those who inhabit these areas whether it is a professional obligation to do so or not.

(2) Our Responsibility to our global environment:

Our planet is our only home. It is all we have to provide us with the material we use to get through life and keep us sustained. One of the worst ills of our modern-day society is that we continuously reap vast amounts of natural sources from the earth for our consumption without regard to the impact this has on the global environment.

It is true we need certain materials to survive and withstand nature. However, in all things there must be moderation and consideration for the ultimate outcome of an act. In the process of creating goods and supplies we destroy whole tracts of land, pollute the ground, water, and air; kill hundreds of millions of animals daily and put a strain on the planets ability to sustain humanity.

We must begin to be mindful of how our actions are affecting our planet and adopt a global mindset where it is understood we must take care of our planet, and not just exploit its sources for economic gain. Know your immediate actions influence the whole. This is our only home and it is our responsibility to care for and maintain it.

The earth is not here for us to exploit and plunder for our pleasure. It is our home and our only one. Let us keep this environment clean and suitable for our use.

———————

Living with creative intent involves taking responsibility for yourself, your peers, your society, and your planet. If you want the best environments and circumstances, then you must actively work toward bringing that about. It is a personal and group effort.

Part 8

Epilogue

"Igni Natura Renovatur Integra"

- Through fire nature is reborn whole

I.   A message to the reader:

"The problems of the world cannot be faced
With the same level of
Consciousness
That created them."

-Albert Einstein

The above quoted statement from one of the greatest minds of our time reveals a truth so profound and simple many who read it still do not believe in its authenticity. Simply stated, it means that your external conditions will not change unless, and until, your internal condition changes. This entails the changing of your thinking, feeling, and actions from the inside out. This truth applies to the individual and to humanity.

The state and condition of the environments and circumstances of the individual, and collective, reflect the conditions of the inner psycho-emotional makeup of the individual and collective. Our outer world corresponds to our inner world. All the world's conflicts and wars are an outward manifestation of the inner conflicts the individuals involved in are experiencing.

The condition of our world is a direct result of humanities choices in the aggregate. One of the main reasons this work was created was to present this fact, and to also demonstrate that this condition-whatever it may be-can be changed if desired. You can change your inner and outer conditions by becoming conscious of this fact, and then acting to change these conditions through conscious intent.

This is one of the reasons for our existence: To evolve through change. The more you change for the better, the more you add to the betterment of the species. An increased consciousness heightens the possibility of true and positive change in your life. You must be conscious of the fact you are responsible for changing your state of mind and being through the power of choice.

Choose to think differently, act differently and see the world in a different light. Choose to choose more wisely. Choose a better life for yourself. Choose to be around good people. Choose to educate yourself. If you feel you are in a good state, then choose to help someone else get there. Be willing to help those who try to help themselves.

For those who are unwilling to change, offer a helping hand. If they are still unwilling to change accept the fact and know that you tried. After that leave and continue your way. Choose to be the best human you can be. Our acts are outward manifestations of the quality of our inner content. How you act, speak, and conduct yourself reflects how you think.

Body language is nearly 90% of language spoken. Its full duty is to express the thoughts and ideas of the other 10% of language unseen in your mind. This is the language of your thoughts. Your thoughts create your actions, and your actions create the circumstances and environments you experience. Once you change your thinking, you can change how you act- and react- to the environments you find yourself in.

You will also see your environments begin to change as well. Once you have developed control over your thoughts and actions you can use this ability to steer your acts towards a more direct and intentional aim. This is where you begin to create your life as you want. This is living with creative intent. When you begin to do this, you can start to develop a good sense of where you are going by analyzing what is being done in the present.

It is the inference derived from the instant acts that give an idea of future events. This is the ability you have. You can consciously bring about future events through the careful application of specific acts in the present. The projects can manifest over a great period in small increments. This is what is known as the concept of gradualism.

Gradualism is the process of manifesting great change in your life through small incremental actions over a period. However, know that there is danger here as it involves the generation of power. With all form of power, a strong sense of responsibility must be developed in order not to abuse that power. Power corrupts and even the most honest of souls can be tempted to take a bite out of the forbidden fruit.

It is your responsibility to use this power wisely and positively. The power to manifest what you desire in life through choice, and taking responsibility for the effects of those choices, must not only be used to benefit you, but to the benefit of humanity as well. One of the biggest shortcomings of humankind is that we have forgotten our duty to each other.

This duty stems from the fact that we all come from the same source on earth as well as in the universe. Everything is connected. Everything is all and one at the same time. This being the case, whatever affects one part affects the whole. Humanity will rise together, and we will fall together. It is everyone's responsibility to use their conscious choice to make decisions that will help to bring about favorable circumstances on this planet.

Look at the events in this world and look at those in your own life. We are all in the same struggle. Know that your choices not only affect your own life, but the lives of others. This is true regarding how the decisions of others affect you as well. So, looking at this in a grand scale you will see the state of the planet and all the lives of those is the sum of the choices made by humanity.

It follows that if people started making better choices and being mindful of how those choices affect not only themselves, but others, then the state of the planet could be changed by making better choices. We must make better choices in our lives. Humanity has been crying out for change for over a millennium.

At each age, there is a different life-threatening issue that hovers over mankind where we ask for intervention to change things for the better. What people have failed to understand is that it is us who must make this change. We are responsible for making great changes on this earth. The archives of humanity reveal the presence on this earth of a large amount of men and women who have tried to help lead the people of this planet toward a better way of life. Some have been successful. Others have not.

Despite the greatness of spiritual strength those people have shown, and the advancements we have all benefitted from as a result, humanity still has a long way to go. The leadership of the past was enough to get us where we are now. It is not enough to get us any further. For humanity to progress any further from here on end, it is going to take a lot more than a single spiritual leader.

It is going to take the efforts of all of humanity working together for a common purpose. We all must be leaders in this new age and take the responsibility of changing the world for the better into our own hands. The responsibility for carrying our race to the next stage of our evolutionary and spiritual unfoldment is ours and ours alone. A single person cannot and will not do this. We must do it together.

The Mayan prediction of the end of the world in 2012 did not entail the end and destruction of our physical planet. It presented the truth that 2012 was the beginning of a time where humanity would have the opportunity to change the belief systems that have shaped ourselves and the world we live in. It was predicted that the time and window of opportunity to do so would begin the end of 2012.

The only thing that was predicted to come to an end was our current way of thinking. Our way of thinking has led to both the good and bad that humanity has experienced over the millennia. Changing our negative thought patterns will change everything associated with those thoughts and end their effects. This is a time and opportunity for us to reinvent ourselves and reach our full potential.

This is our time to work toward a more positive and sustainable way of living. Everyone on this planet has the potential to reach their full potential. We just have to make the choice to do so and act upon that choice. In addition to this, everyone on earth is involved in this process of global change. Everyone has a part to play and is responsible for contributing to the process. Just remember if you are not part of the solution, you are part of the problem.

It appears the main obstacle to this process is that we spend too much time obtaining and very little on becoming. We do not spend enough time working on ourselves to develop our selves spiritually or morally and fail to mature as a result. This must be changed. We have become enslaved by all we have created. The systems we created to help us get goods, amenities, pleasure, and comfort have enslaved us.

We must change this. This can begin by changing how you think. Adopt the mindset that life is about more than just making money to buy stuff. Life is about evolution toward a higher state of being mentally and spiritually. Slowly but surely, the bonds that were created which hold us back in life will begin to break away and free us from their yoke. You can create a new reality here on earth through the power of creative intent.

The purpose of this book is to teach you that you can make this happen. do so by starting with yourself. It's you that must make it happen. The responsibility for changing ourselves, our lives, the lives of others, and all on this earth lies solely within mankind. Do not wait for someone else to do for you what you must do for yourself.

Do not wait for a circumstance to change that you are not actively working toward changing. Do not wait for some great intervention from an outside source to solve all the world's problems.

You are the world's savior. You are the sole solution to all the problems existing in this world today. You, and the human species are the solution to the world's problems as its humanity that has created them. You are the change that is so desperately needed.

It is known that the lives of many are filled with great suffering and sadness. We have all had experiences in our lives both positive and negative. We all share in the same struggles of life no matter where you are, or who you are. Everyone has joys and pains. This stems from what we have experienced.

What we experience shapes the way we think and how we think creates the circumstances we experience. It is a cycle of positive reinforcement. We create the causes of our experiences through our choices. One of the greatest secrets to begin changing our thought processes is the utilization of the power of forgiveness.

Forgiveness in this sense is not intended to absolve the offender of the burden of accepting responsibility for their acts but frees the victim from the psycho-emotional disturbances caused by the attachment to the feelings caused by the offensive act. Forgiveness helps heal our trauma. Forgiveness detaches the mind and body from ill feelings. This frees the person from the grip of ill will and resentment and allows the mind to focus on more positive things in life.

Moreover, the anger felt at an injustice should be directed toward the act and not the actor. We are human and as such make many mistakes in life. Most of them have a bad impact on others as well as our-selves. This is due mostly to ignorance. We are all human and all have yet to reach the top of our full potential. We have yet to reach the pinnacle of perfection in human thought and behavior.

As such, for the duration of time we travel on the path toward that goal we will continuously err and make mistakes. Sometimes our mistakes will hurt ourselves. Sometimes they hurt others. Nonetheless, no matter what happens, let the anger be reflected at the act not the actor, and be willing to forgive. For oft times we are unaware of what we do and its affect's on others.

If only we were aware of the exact consequences of the act the moment we chose to commit it and saw the effects of our actions on ourselves and others would we choose to do differently. It is our responsibility to ensure we are mindful of what we do and take heed to our faults in order to ensure the causes of all erroneous behavior are eliminated in ourselves and others.

Never allow yourself to succumb to hatred for your brothers, or sisters. Educate yourself as to the causes of events and turn your hatred of the trials of life into wisdom and understanding of their meaning and purpose. This process begins by educating yourself, being mindful of your actions and thoughts, and incorporating love as a major part of your life. Love is the tool that will allow you to eliminate hurt and pain from yourself.

It gives you the strength to help others relieve themselves of their hurt and pain. It is the way in which you bridge the gap that has been built up between the peoples of this planet. It appears we have forgotten that we come from the same source of being and creation, regardless of your idea of what this is.

Modern day scientific studies of mitochondrial DNA, which is a DNA strand transferred from mother to child, have revealed that all human beings, and their ancestry can bio-genetically be traced back to a common ancestral lineage. This lineage is traced back to over 6 million years. This means we not only have the same earth mother, but a biological mother as well. As such we are all brothers and sisters. We are the human family in its most literal sense.

Just like a family we fuss with each other and have our moments, but we must also work together like a family for the common purpose of advancing our species. Society itself is a direct result of our ancestors' realization that the only way they were going to survive against nature and her elements was to work together for the common benefit of all. This means they stuck together, and that is the only reason why we are still here today.

Over the course of human evolution humanity has lived in a state of hunter-gatherer, to small bands and tribes, clans, towns, city-states, nations, and empires. This was done by working together. Despite their differences, those people achieved great things on this earth. They have likewise done some bad things; The point is we must take the next step together.

It is time to take the next step together in our human evolution and unite as a people in the world. This does not entail the eradication of national or personal identities, but the conscious establishment of the fact we are all in this together and will benefit greatly if we all worked together toward a common goal. It is our responsibility to actively engage in this great work together. Allow this truth to impress your consciousness.

Plant the seed of unity in your mind, so that you may be able to use your mind to create a greater world. Look at all that has been done with the conscious use of only 10% of your brain. Just imagine if we could develop our minds and access more of it. The ability to collectively use 10, 15, or 20% of our minds would allow us to achieve a great amount of good in the world.

You must take the first step. We all do. Choose to let go of the negativity that has held you back. Let go of all the bad that has been adversely affecting you and holding you back. Look at all you do from your speech to your acts, and even your thoughts. Get rid of whatever does not contribute to something good. Choose to be the change you want in the world, and the change you want to see in others.

It has been written in many religious texts of a prophesied battle that will take place on this earth that will mark the end of humanity. This epic battle, known as Armageddon, world war 3, and many other names is simply a resolution of the conflict between the positive and negative poles of human nature. It is the age-old battle between good and evil taking place within us. As human beings, we possess both good and evil within us.

The manifestation of either depends upon our understanding of their purpose and what we allow to manifest through us. The vast majority of ills present are the result of the imbalance of these poles within us. Therefore, we can see the most divinely inspired acts come from human beings, and the most vile and evil.

We have lost control of these natures within ourselves due to the failure to remember that not only do they exist within us, but it is our responsibility to control and balance them. Which aspect of these forces dominate in an individual can be discerned through an observation of the acts of the individual. The key to controlling these natures lie within the use of the mind. He we come full circle. The mind is the key to it all. Our conscious mind decides what goes into it and what doesn't.

It absorbs information, processes it, and then makes a judgement as to what action to take. This is why establishing harmony within ourselves has been so difficult. It is because it is an internal struggle that must be fought using the same tools that created the problems in the first place. The only tool you have is your mind. You must change your thinking to change your life and the lives of others.

You must be mindful of what you allow to enter your mind, and of the effect it will have on you. How you think affects you and everyone in this world. We are all connected through the common blood lineage and through a collective unconscious. Our collective unconscious is an Akashik record which holds all our experiences, struggles, desires, and history. This collective unconscious binds us psychologically, emotionally, energetically, and spiritually.

This means if one of us are suffering, all of us are suffering. Just look at an individual when he is sick. When the part of the body affected is not functioning correctly, the whole body does not function correctly. If the cause of any whole is to be searched for a malfunction the parts of that whole must be examined. In order to discover the causes of ills for humanity it is the individuals who must be looked at for the basis of those causes.

We are all united in a common struggle against our own nature but can only succeed at overcoming this struggle individually. This is the great battle that must be fought and won if we are to survive as a species. It can be won, but only if we all win. It can be done. Humanity, together and individually, has the power to overcome the negative nature that exists within us.

Overcoming the negative nature within us does not entail the destruction of it, but the transmutation of that which is bad within us into something good, and not letting the bad influence corrupt us. This is the meaning of partaking of the wisdom of the serpent, but not of its nature.

This process of change will lead humanity down the next step and stage of our evolution.

The time to act is now. Those that came before us struggled against many adversities to get us to the point of advancement in civilization and technology we are at now. The ball has been passed onto our current generation. It is our responsibility to continue this work in order that our descendants experience a fuller and more meaningful life the result of a higher quality of living created by us.

The responsibility for creating a better world for our-selves and upcoming generations is ours and ours alone. We are the savior we have been waiting for. The responsibility to bring about global change is ours. It is your responsibility as an individual to do your part in making this world

a better place by making yourself a better person.

You need to make the choice to improve your

life to improve the lives of those around you. It is

the responsibility of all humanity to work toward

a better future by working to improve the present

circumstances and improving the state of our

global environment, social environment, and

personal environment. Remember that our

greatest asset and tool to utilize in this process is

our minds, in proper balance with the inclinations

of our hearts.

The source of spiritual energy that will fuel

this process is derived from love. Every day you

live must be spent in the presence of love. The

power of love must govern our actions and act as

a guide in all our endeavors. Love is the staple

that reconciles all differences and binds all material and immaterial aspects of our reality together.

Upon an informed examination, you will discover energy and matter are one and the same. In fact, there is no such thing as matter. Albert Einstein's equation $E=MC^2$ demonstrates energy is the equivalent of mass accelerated to the speed of light squared. The opposite is also true. Matter is the result of the decrease of the speed of light energy to the point where it appears to materialize in tangible form.

Increase the vibratory rate of the atomic particles of material objects to the speed of light squared, and that material object will de-materialize and become pure energy. Decrease the vibratory rate of energy under the speed of light squared and that energy will materialize into a concrete object whose level of solidity will correspond to the vibratory rate it stopped at.

If energy and mass are the same, and our mind operates as a conscious energetic substance that functions at about the equivalent of 12 watts of power, then it logically follows we can direct this flow of energy toward changing material events by using our mind to focus this energy with intentional aim.

When using your mind with conscious intent, and allowing love to be your guide, you will be able to increase the power of your mind and body. You will develop a stronger ability to govern the two, and events in your life. You are a living, breathing symbol of the force and energy that pervades the universe. You are physical consciousness. As such you have the power of choice inherited from the source of your creation to determine what you want to create in life.

You are blessed in all ways to have the opportunity to experience love in motion. This love is life itself. Do not waste this blessing by violating life. Do not make choices that will drive you and those around you into a sea of destruction and decadence. It would be a great disrespect to this miracle of creation.

Use the power of positive choice to honor yourself and life. Use the power of your choice to bring about paradise in your life and those around you. Use the power of choice to protect and preserve the health and beauty of this planet we call home. Choose to make a positive

difference in your life.

Intentionally create the best version of your life

and yourself

It is your responsibility; no one else's.

Choose wisely.